Handbook for
Differential Diagnosis
of Neurologic
Signs and Symptoms

Handbook for Differential Diagnosis of Neurologic Signs and Symptoms

KENNETH M. HEILMAN, M.D.,
Professor, Department of Neurology,
University of Florida College of Medicine,
Gainesville, Florida

ROBERT T. WATSON, M.D.,
Associate Professor, Department of Neurology,
University of Florida College of Medicine,
Gainesville, Florida

MELVIN GREER, M.D.,
Professor and Chairman, Department of Neurology,
University of Florida College of Medicine,
Gainesville, Florida

APPLETON-CENTURY-CROFTS/New York

Library of Congress Cataloging in Publication Data

Heilman, Kenneth M   1938-
    Handbook for differential diagnosis of neurologic
signs and symptoms.

    1.   Nervous system—Diseases—Diagnosis.
2.   Diagnosis, Differential.   3.   Neurologic manifestations of general diseases.   I.   Watson,
Robert T., joint author.   II.   Greer, Melvin, joint
author.   III.   Title. [DNLM: 1.   Nervous system
diseases—Diagnosis—Tables.   2.   Neurologic examination—Tables.   WL16 H466h]
RC348.H397   616.8'94'75   77-2589
ISBN 0-8385-3617-4

Prentice-Hall International, Inc., London
Prentice-Hall of Australia, Pty. Ltd., Sydney
Prentice-Hall of India Private Limited, New Delhi
Prentice-Hall of Japan, Inc., Tokyo
Prentice-Hall of Southeast Asia (Pte.) Ltd., Singapore
Whitehall Books, Wellington, New Zealand

PRINTED IN THE UNITED STATES OF AMERICA

DEDICATED TO OUR FAMILIES

Preface

This handbook is designed to serve as a problem-oriented guide to the physician who is caring for patients with neurologic diseases. The traditional neurology texts are usually organized by disease states and their underlying etiology and pathology (eg, infectious diseases, neoplastic diseases, vascular diseases). Since the clinician frequently does not have a priori knowledge of the etiology of his patients' complaints, these books are of limited help in guiding him to the correct diagnosis. This problem-oriented text has been designed to assist the clinician through the deductive process needed to make an accurate diagnosis.

Unlike the traditional text, this problem-oriented guide does not review the natural history of the disease, the pathology, the prognosis, and many other aspects of specific diseases. After the clinician has made a diagnosis, it is important for him to know as much as possible about a specific disease. We would suggest that this handbook be used in conjunction with a standard neurology text. Finally, although we discuss treatment, prior to treating a patient with a pharmacologic agent the physician should acquaint himself with doses, indications and contraindications, side effects, and other aspects of the proposed treatment.

Contents

Preface

Chapter 1   Episodic Disorders   1

  1. Differential Diagnosis of Headaches   4
  2. Differential Diagnosis of Vascular Headaches   5
  3. Treatment of Tension and Migraine Headaches   6
  4. Differential Diagnosis of Seizures and Syncope   6
  5. Principal Causes of Syncope   7
  6. Classification of Seizures   8
  7. Distinguishing Features of Some Paroxysmal Events in Children   9
  8. Etiology of Seizures by Age Group   10
  9. Electroencephalographic Abnormalities   12
 10. Evaluation of Seizures   13
 11. Drugs Used in Treatment of Seizures   14
 12. Pharmacologic Properties of Drugs Used in Treatment
     of Seizures   16
 13. Treatment of Status Epilepticus (Adult)   16

Chapter 2   Weakness   17

  1. Differential Diagnosis Between Upper and Lower
     Motor Neuron Disease   21
  2. Differential Diagnosis of Upper Motor Neuron Weakness   22
  3. Diseases That May Produce Hemispheric Weakness in
     the Adult   23
     Figure 1. Pathologic Anatomy Underlying Myelopathy   24
  4. Signs and Symptoms Associated with Various Forms
     of Myelopathy   25
  5. Diseases That May Produce Myelopathy   26
  6. Clinical Differential Diagnosis of Motor Unit Weakness   29

7. Laboratory Differential Diagnosis of Motor Unit Weakness   30
8. Motor Neuropathies and Amyotrophies   31
9. Diseases of Spinal Roots (Radiculopathy)   34
10. Common Root Syndromes   36
11. Segmental Innervation of Muscles and Motor Function   37
12. Differential Diagnosis of Neuropathy by Major Clinical Signs   44
13. Differential Diagnosis of Neuropathy by Etiology   45
14. Compression and Entrapment Neuropathies   56
15. Laboratory Studies in Neuropathy   59
16. Differential Diagnosis of Diseases Affecting the
      Myoneural Junction   60
17. Differential Diagnosis of Major Etiologies of Muscle
      Disease   61
18. Differential Diagnosis of Dystrophy   62
19. Differential Diagnosis of Benign Congenital Myopathies   64
20. Differential Diagnosis of Myositis   65
21. Differential Diagnosis of Endocrine Myopathies   67
22. Differential Diagnosis of Periodic Paralysis   68
23. Differential Diagnosis of Myoglobinuria   69

Chapter 3   **Sensory Defects**   **70**

Figure 2A. Dermatome Map, Anterior   72
Figure 2B. Dermatome Map, Posterior   73
Figure 3.   Dermatome Map   74
Figure 4A. Cutaneous Fields of Peripheral Nerves From
      Anterior Aspect   75
Figure 4B. Cutaneous Fields of Peripheral Nerves From
      Posterior Aspect   76
1. Diseases That Produce Pain Insensitivity and Hereditary
      Sensory Neuropathies   77

Chapter 4   **Abnormalities of Tone, Posture, Coordination,
and Movement**   **78**

1. Differential Diagnosis of Dystonia   83
2. Sites of Some Muscle Cramp States   85
3. Etiology of Muscle Cramps   86
4. Treatment of Muscle Cramps   87
5. Persistent Muscle Contraction Syndromes   88
6. Differentiating Features of Increased Tone in Myopathies,
      Tetany, Rigidity, and Persistent Muscle Contraction States   89
7. Differential Diagnosis of Diseases That Cause Athetosis   91
8. Differential Diagnosis of Chorea   92
9. Differential Diagnosis of Ballismus   93
10. Differential Diagnosis of Tremor   94
11. Etiology of Tremor   95
12. Treatment of Abnormal Movements   96

13. Differential Diagnosis of Some Diseases That Produce
    Cerebellar Signs and Symptoms   97
14. Familial and Hereditary Diseases with Cerebellar Signs   99
15. Etiologies of Segmental Myoclonus   101
16. Differential Diagnosis of Generalized Myoclonus   102
17. Laboratory Studies in Myoclonus   104
18. Major Gait Disorders   105

Chapter 5   Coma   107

1. Diagnostic Studies   108
2. Level of Dysfunction   109
3. Differential Diagnosis Between Metabolic and Structural
   Causes of Coma   110
4. Coma from Causes Other Than Mass Lesions   111
5. Structural Causes of Coma   112

Chapter 6   Behavior Disorders   114

1. Types of Memory Disorders   118
2. Etiology of Dementias   119
3. Laboratory Evaluation of Dementia   120
4. Aphasic Disorders   121

Chapter 7   Autonomic Disorders   123

1. Autonomic Disorders   124
2. Differential Diagnosis of Neurogenic Bladder   126
   Figure 5. Sites of Lesions in Neurogenic Bladder   128

Chapter 8   Increased Intracranial Pressure   129

1. Diseases That May Produce Increased Intracranial
   Pressure: Clinical Features   132
2. Differential Diagnosis of Increased Intracranial Pressure:
   Laboratory Studies   143

Chapter 9   Cranial Nerve Dysfunction   151

1. Cranial Nerves   160
   Figure 6. Anatomy Underlying Common Brainstem
     Syndromes   164
   Figure 7. Autonomic Neuroanatomy of Pupillary Control   167
2. Classic Brainstem Syndromes   168
3. Factors That May Produce Defects in Olfaction   170
4. Unilateral Visual Loss   171
5. Optic Atrophy   172
6. Differentiation of Papilledema, Optic Neuritis, and
   Retrobulbar Neuritis   174
7. Common Visual Field Defects   175
8. Etiology of Diplopia   177
9. Dysfunction of Cranial Nerve V   178
10. Site of Cranial Nerve VII Disruption   180

11. Etiology of Cranial Nerve VII Dysfunction   182
12. Causes of Deafness   183
13. Localization of Hearing Defects   184
14. Causes of Dizziness   185
15. Differentiating Features of Some Common Causes of
    Dizziness   187
16. Types of Nystagmus   188
17. Diseases Affecting the Lower Four Cranial Nerves   189

Chapter 10 Stiff Neck   **190**

1. Cerebrospinal Fluid Findings in Stiff Neck   193
2. Causes of Depressed Cerebrospinal Fluid Glucose   196
3. Causes of Cerebrospinal Fluid Lymphocytosis   197
4. Antibiotic Treatment for Bacterial Meningitis   198
5. Evaluation of Probable Meningitis   199
6. Evaluation of Suspected Hemorrhage   200

Chapter 11 Apoplexy   **201**

1. Etiology of Stroke   202
2. Differential Diagnosis between Hemorrhage and Infarction   203
3. Differential Diagnosis between Intracerebral and
   Subarachnoid Hemorrhage   203
4. Differential Diagnosis of Hemorrhages   204
5. Differential Diagnosis between Embolus and Thrombosis   205
6. Differential Diagnosis and Treatment of Infarction   205

Chapter 12 Cerebral Palsy and Hypotonia of Infancy   **206**

1. Types of Cerebral Palsy   208
2. Causes of Temporary Hypotonia   210
3. Causes of Permanent Hypotonia   210

Chapter 13 Abnormal Head Size   **211**

1. Types of Premature Suture Closure   212
2. Etiology of Macrocrania   213
3. Investigative Techniques for Macrocrania   214
4. Etiology of Microcrania   215

Chapter 14 Mental Deficiency   **216**

1. Causes of Static Mental Deficiency   219
2. Tests for Static Causes of Mental Deficiency   220
3. Dysmorphic Conditions and Chromosomal Abnormalities
   Associated with Static Causes of Mental Deficiency   221
4. Signs and Symptoms of Progressive Disorders Causing
   Mental Deficiency   223
5. Causes of Progressive Mental Deficiency   224
6. Laboratory Studies in Progressive Neurologic Diseases
   Associated with Mental Deficiency   231

Handbook for
Differential Diagnosis
of Neurologic
Signs and Symptoms

1
Episodic Disorders

HEADACHES

Headache is one of the most common neurologic complaints. Headache is defined as pain distributed in the upper region of the head (from orbits to suboccipital region).

In the head there are a limited number of pain-sensitive structures: (1) scalp and neck muscles; (2) blood vessels (eg, dural arteries, large arteries at the base of the brain, scalp vessels, dural sinuses); (3) nerves (including V, IX, X, and upper cervical nerves). These structures produce pain when they are stretched, compressed, dilated, or inflamed. In general, pain from intracranial structures above the superior surface of the tentorium is referred to the anterior portion of the head, and pain from intracranial structures below the tentorium is referred to the occipital and suboccipital regions.

There are five major types of headaches: (1) vascular headaches, (2) muscle contraction headaches, (3) traction headaches, (4) headache of cranial inflammation, and (5) extracranial headaches. In the evaluation of a patient with headache, it is important to diagnose which type of headache the patient is having; the differential diagnosis is outlined in Table 1. After diagnosing the major group, then consideration of the differential diagnosis within each group can be undertaken (Table 2).

A complete history and physical and neurologic evaluation should be performed for every patient with headache. Frequently it will be found that

1

further laboratory tests are not needed to make the diagnosis of migraine or tension headache. However, if one diagnoses tension headache and the pain is anterior, then one may want to obtain sinus films to help rule out sinusitis. Intraocular pressure measurements should be obtained to rule out glaucoma. In addition to sinusitis, muscle contraction headaches are commonly confused with traction headaches. If one wishes to rule out traction headaches, a computerized axial tomography (CAT) scan is the best screening test. In the absence of the apparatus necessary for a CAT scan, a brain scan and EEG should help exclude a mass lesion.

Recurrent migraine that always occurs on the same side may occasionally be caused by an arteriovenous malformation. A dynamic brain scan is a good screening test. If one suspects nonmigrainous vascular headache, then blood gasses and serum glucose should be obtained. Every patient should have blood pressure determinations. When vascular headaches are confused with other types of headaches, they are most frequently confused with headaches of cranial inflammation. If one suspects that cranial inflammation is producing a headache, then the patient should have a lumbar puncture (LP). Any patient with sudden onset of severe headache with or without loss of consciousness (without focal neurologic signs) should have an LP to rule out a subarachnoid hemorrhage. Patients over 50 years of age should have a determination of erythrocyte sedimentation rate to rule out temporal arteritis.

When possible, one should treat headaches of cranial inflammation (see Chap. 10), nonmigrainous vascular headaches, traction headaches (see Chap. 8), and extracranial headaches by treating the underlying disease. Treatment of tension headache and migraine headache is presented in Table 3. Prior to treatment the physician should familiarize himself with indications, contraindications, adverse effects, and dosages of the medications to be used.

SYNCOPE

Syncope is defined as a temporary loss of consciousness. Usually there is no permanent neuropathology associated with this loss of consciousness. Although syncope is frequently associated with self-limited and benign conditions, it may be a symptom of a serious underlying disease. Sudden loss of consciousness, in addition to being socially troublesome, may lead to serious injury. Therefore patients with syncope should be carefully evaluated. In the differential diagnosis of syncope, one first must be certain that one is dealing with syncope (no neuropathology), as opposed to the brief loss of consciousness that can be associated with seizures. Seizures often denote underlying neuropathology, and they must be worked up in a different manner (see following section). The differential diagnosis between seizures and syncope is covered in Table 4.

After it is decided that one is dealing with syncope and not seizures, then the differential diagnosis of syncope (Table 5) must be considered. The history is of paramount importance. Unless a patient is having transient cranial nerve signs, it is difficult to make the diagnosis of basilar artery insufficiency. Syncope may be the only symptom of migraine, but frequently migraine is associated with other signs (see previous section). If syncope is being caused by a subarachnoid hemorrhage, there may be other signs such as headache (see previous section) or stiff neck. Lumbar puncture may be diagnostic. The history may also be helpful if the patient states that he passes out when he stands up quickly, has skipping of his heartbeat, or passes out after he turns his head, urinates, or coughs. A physical examination with special attention to the cardiovascular system will help to ascertain if syncope is being caused by a cardiovascular disease.

Laboratory studies such as chest x-ray, EKG, cardiac monitoring, blood glucose determination, and drug screens may also be helpful in determining the etiology of syncope.

Therapy should be aimed at the underlying disease.

SEIZURE DISORDERS

Seizures may be symptoms of (1) genetic predisposition to neuronal excitability, (2) metabolic abnormalities, or (3) focal pathology of the central nervous system. The classification of seizures can be found in Table 6. Frequently, seizures can be confused with syncope (see Table 4), and in children, seizures can be confused with breath-holding spells (see Table 7).

In each age group there are different diseases that may produce seizures. The principal causes of seizures in different groups can be found in Table 8. Frequently the clinician may need laboratory studies to help him in the differential diagnosis. An EEG is one of the most important tests in helping to differentiate the different types of seizures (see Table 9). Table 10 is a flowchart of how a patient with a seizure disorder should be evaluated.

In regard to treatment, there are six major principles: (1) Start with one drug. (2) Increase the dosage until the patient is either seizure-free or shows evidence of toxicity. (3) Add a second drug if necessary. (4) Change the dosage only after a trial lasting a minimum of 1 week. (5) Do not terminate medication unless the patient is seizure-free for at least 2 years. (6) It is also helpful if blood levels can be obtained. The drugs used in the treatment of seizures can be found in Table 11; their pharmacologic properties are listed in Table 12. The treatment of status epilepticus can be found in Table 13.

TABLE 1

Differential Diagnosis of Headaches

MANIFESTATIONS	VASCULAR HEADACHE	MUSCLE CONTRACTION HEADACHE	TRACTION HEADACHE	CRANIAL INFLAMMATION HEADACHE	EXTRACRANIAL HEADACHE
Laterality	Usually unilateral onset	Usually bilateral	Unilateral or bilateral	Bilateral	Unilateral or bilateral
Severity	Severe	Mild to severe	Usually mild	Severe	Mild to severe
Throbbing	Present at onset	Usually absent at onset, but may be present during peak	Usually absent	Present	Usually absent
Change with head position	Severe	Mild	Moderate	Severe	Mild
Time course	Acute	Subacute to chronic	Subacute to chronic	Acute	Acute to subacute
Gastrointestinal disturbance	Severe	Absent or mild	Moderate	Mild to severe	Absent
Visual disturbance	Present	Absent	May be present	May be present	Absent
Tenderness	Mild over extracranial vessels	Severe in suboccipital and temporalis muscles	Absent	Absent except in temporal arteries	Present in sinusitis
Focal neurologic signs	May be present	Absent	May be present	May be present	Absent
Stiff neck	Absent	Mild	Mild to severe	Severe	Absent

TABLE 2

Differential Diagnosis of Vascular Headaches

MIGRAINE HEADACHES

Classic migraine: contralateral neurologic symptoms (eg, hemanopsia, scotoma, amblyopia, paresthesia, numbness, weakness, speech disturbances) are followed by a unilateral throbbing headache that lasts several hours and is associated with nausea and vomiting. Frequently there is a strong family history

Common migraine: unilateral or bilateral throbbing headache without neurologic manifestations

Ophthalmologic migraine: ophthalmoplegia may occur after headache, which is on same side as eye findings

Cluster headache (histamine cephalagia, Horton's headache): severe unilateral pain that frequently arouses patient from sleep and is associated with unilateral lacrimation, conjunctival injection, ptosis, miosis, and nasal stuffiness; these headaches come in a series or in clusters, and pain is mainly in the eye and temporal regions

NONMIGRAINOUS VASCULAR HEADACHES

Changes in blood composition
  Hypercapnia
  Hypoxia
  Hypoglycemia
  Carbon monoxide

Drug-induced
  Nitrates
  Caffeine withdrawal
  Hangover

Other
  Post convulsion
  Post seizure
  Fever
  Hypertension

TABLE 3

Treatment of Migraine and Tension Headaches

TREATMENT	MIGRAINE HEADACHE	MUSCLE CONTRACTION HEADACHE
Vasoactive agents	Ergot preparations (eg, ergotamine tartrate)	Not useful
Analgesics	(1) Acetaminophen or (2) acetylsalicylic acid (ASA) or (3) Fiorinal or other analgesics	Same as migraine
Prophylaxis	(1) D/C oral contraceptives; (2) propranolol or (3) cyproheptadine HCl (Periactin) or (4) methysergide maleate (Sansert) or (5) low-tyramine diet	Muscle relaxants, eg, diazepam (Valium), or mood elevators, eg, amitriptyline HCl (Elavil)
Behavioral-Mechanical	Biofeedback, psychotherapy	Biofeedback (EMG), relaxation exercises; psychotherapy
Other	For nausea and vomiting, perchlorperazine (Compazine) or trimethobenzamide (Tigan)	—

TABLE 4

Differential Diagnosis of Seizures and Syncope

	SEIZURES	SYNCOPE
Motor activity	Tonic rigidity, clonic activity, mouth movement, automatic behavior	Usually limp without movements
Injuries	Tongue-biting and injuries secondary to clonic activity	Injuries secondary to fall
Incontinence	Present with major motor seizure	Usually absent
Cry	Usually at beginning of major motor seizure	Absent
Changes in respiration	Usually associated with tonic-clonic activity	May increase or decrease with syncope caused by changes in blood composition
Pulse	Usually increased	May decrease or may be irregular
Postictal lethargy	May be present	Absent
Postictal neurologic sign	May be present	Absent
EEG	May be abnormal	Should be normal (when patient is not unconscious)

TABLE 5

Principal Causes of Syncope

CENTRAL NERVOUS SYSTEM
Hysteria

LOCAL ISCHEMIA OF CENTRAL NERVOUS SYSTEM
Basilar artery insufficiency
Migraine
Subarachnoid hemorrhage

GENERALIZED FALL IN BLOOD PRESSURE
Vasovagal
Carotid sinus
Aortic valvular disease
Myocardial infarction
Pulmonary embolus
Dissecting aneurysm
Orthostatic hypotension
Arrhythmia
Atrial myxoma
Cough syncope
Urination syncope

CHANGES IN BLOOD COMPOSITION
Hypercapnia
Hypoglycemia
Hypoxia
Hypocapnia
Drugs

TABLE 6

Classification of Seizures

PARTIAL SEIZURES

The focal clinical features are from activation of a specific group of neurons with a correlative focal EEG abnormality. These phenomena may remain focal or may become generalized, and there is usually an underlying pathologic substrate. The onset may be at any age, and there may be a focal abnormality on routine examination or a postictal focal abnormality

> *With elementary symptoms*: usually no generalization and therefore no loss of consciousness
> > Motor (Jacksonian, adversive, aphasic, etc)
> > Sensory (somatic. visual, auditory, olfactory, vertiginous, etc)
> > Autonomic (rare)
> > Compound (combined elementary and/or complex symptoms)
>
> *With complex symptoms*: corresponds to temporal lobe (psychomotor) epilepsy that usually leads to impaired consciousness; may have elementary onset
> > Only impaired consciousness
> > Cognitive (déjà vu, forced thinking, etc)
> > Affective
> > Psychosensory (hallucinations, macropsia, etc)
> > Psychomotor automatisms
> > Combinations
>
> *Partial seizures secondarily generalized*: usually tonic-clonic seizure developing from a partial seizure

GENERALIZED SEIZURES

These are without local onset. There is usually initial loss of consciousness with generalized motor findings and an EEG correlate of bilateral synchronous discharge

> *Primary*: absence of etiology and presumed genetic in origin; examination usually normal; onset usually in childhood or adolescence, with persistence to adulthood
> > Absence (petit mal)
> > > Simple: only impaired consciousness
> > > Complex: impaired consciousness with one or more of the following:
> > > > Mild clonic movements (myoclonic absences)
> > > > Increased postural tone (retropulsive absence)
> > > > Decreased postural tone (atonic absence)
> > > > Automatisms (automatic absence)
> > > > Autonomic (eg, enuretic)
> > > > Mixed
> > Grand mal
> > Myoclonus (massive bilateral)
>
> *Secondary*: Caused by diffuse cerebral disease with abnormal exam.
> > Atypical petit mal
> > Tonic-clonic (grand mal)
> > Atonic
> > Massive bilateral myoclonus

UNILATERAL

Presents with clinical features restricted to one side of the body with EEG discharge over the contralateral hemisphere. These may be tonic, clonic, or tonic-clonic, with or without impaired consciousness, may shift sides, but do not become symmetrical.

TABLE 7

Distinguishing Features of Some Paroxysmal Events in Children

FEATURE	PETIT MAL	PSYCHOMOTOR	BREATH-HOLDING	FEBRILE CONVULSIONS
Age at onset	4–10 years	Older child, adolescent	3 months to 4 years	Less than 6 years; most occur between 6 months and 3 years
Frequency	Frequent, several per day	Variable, many per day followed by days or weeks free from seizures	Infrequent, but increase to about age 4, when they cease	Infrequent, occurs soon after onset of a fever
Precipitating factor	Hyperventilation, hypoglycemia	Sleep, drugs (eg, Brevital, Thorazine)	Always present (eg, minor injury or emotional upset)	Extracranial infection with fever
Crying	Never	May occur as part of aura	Always precedes	Not precipitating factor
Cyanosis	Never	Never	Always precedes loss of consciousness rather than occurring with loss of consciousness or during major motor convulsive activity	No
Aura	No	Yes	No	No
Tone changes or postictal motor movements	Normal tone, but with eyelid, eyebrow, and hand twitching; rarely, atonic, with falling to floor	Eyelid blinking or fluttering; complex automatisms (eg, lip-smacking, chewing, fumbling); motor onset	Opisthotonos	Grand mal
Postictal lethargy	No	Yes	Sometimes	Yes
Duration	Less than 30 sec	From seconds to several minutes	About 1 minute for consciousness and/or clonic movements	Very brief, to minutes
EEG	Specific	Abnormal, usually focal temporal; may need nasopharyngeal or sphenoidal electrodes to visualize discharge	Normal between events	Normal 1 week after seizure

TABLE 8

Etiology of Seizures, by Age Group

CAUSES	NEONATAL	INFANCY AND CHILDHOOD	ADULT
Toxic-metabolic	Hypoglycemia Hypocalcemia Hypernatremia, hyponatremia Hypomagnesemia Narcotic withdrawal Pyridoxine dependency Pyridoxine deficiency Hyperbilirubinemia Hypoxia Drug withdrawal Cyanotic congenital heart disease Placental abnormalities Maternal toxemia or anoxia Aminoacidurias	Lead Thallium Drugs	Withdrawal from alcohol or barbiturates Picrotoxin Metrazole Strychnine Camphor Arsenic Thallium Lead Organic solvents Hypoglycemia Hypocalcemia or hypoparathyroidism Toxemia

Trauma	Intracranial hemorrhage from
	  birth trauma (intraventricular,
	  subdural, subarachnoid)
		Birth trauma
		Trauma (latent)
			Seizure onset within 2 months to 2 years
			  after initial trauma

Infection	Bacterial meningitis
	Congenital lues
	Cytomegalic inclusion disease
	Congenital toxoplasmosis
	Viral meningoencephalitis
	Maternal rubella
		Same as neonatal
		Subdural empyema
		Abscess
		Parasites
		Allergic reaction to diphtheria, smallpox,
		  and typhoid inoculations
		SSPE
		Subdural effusion
			Encephalitis, especially equine, herpes
			  simplex, St. Louis and California
			Bacterial meningitis
			Fungal
			Lues
			Subdural empyema
			Abscess
			Parasites
			Jakob–Creutzfeldt disease

Etiologic Category			
Congenital or familial	Microgyria Porencephaly Hydranencephaly Vascular anomalies Tuberous sclerosis	Same defects of development as neonatal Unverricht-Lundborg myoclonic epilepsy Tuberous sclerosis Sturge-Weber syndrome	Acute intermittent porphyria
Degenerative		Disorders of protein, carbohydrate, lipids, eg, PKU, Tay-Sachs disease (see Chapter 14) Demyelinating, eg, multiple sclerosis (rarely) and Schilder's disease	Alzheimer's disease Pick's disease Multiple sclerosis
Neoplastic	Rare	Usually in association with neurocutaneous syndromes	Increasing incidence with age; strong consideration in middle-age adult with seizure onset, accounting for 10% of seizures after 20 years of age
Vascular	Anoxia Intraventricular hemorrhage	Arteriovenous malformation Vasculitis Hypertension	Arteriosclerosis (becomes more common past age 50), arteriovenous malformation, vasculitis, hypertension, infarction (embolus is more likely to produce seizures than thrombosis), intracerebral hemorrhage, venous sinus thrombosis, carotid sinus hypersensitivity, Stokes-Adams disease, vasovagal syndrome, postural hypotension

TABLE 9

Electroencephalographic Abnormalities

SEIZURE TYPES	ICTAL EEG	INTERICTAL EEG
Partial Seizures	Local contralateral rhythmic discharge of spikes and/or slow waves starting over the area of cortex corresponding to the symptoms	Intermittent local discharge of spike or spike–wave complexes
Generalized Seizures		
Primary		
Absence (petit mal)	Symmetric 3-cps spike and wave	Normal background rhythm with symmetric bursts of polyspikes or polyspike and wave superimposed; produced by hyperventilation
Grand mal	Symmetric recruiting buildup followed by polyspiking at a frequency of 10 cps or greater during the tonic phase, and slow waves during clonic phase	Normal background rhythm with symmetric polyspike and wave and/or spike and wave or polyspikes superimposed; provoked by hyperventilation, photic stimuli, sleep
Myoclonus–massive	Symmetric polyspike and wave	Symmetric polyspike and wave
Secondary		
Atypical petit mal	Low-voltage fast-activity arrhythmic discharge at 10 cps or more; rhythmic sharp and slow waves sometimes asymmetric; pseudorhythmic spike and wave at 2 cps	Sharp and slow wave discharges, sometimes asymmetric or slow background rhythm
Grand mal	As above	Slow background rhythm with superimposed generalized or asymmetric slow spike and wave discharge
Atonic	Pseudorhythmic 2-cps spike and wave	As above
Myoclonus–massive	Polyspike and wave	As above
Infantile spasms	Continuous multifocal slow waves with intermingled focal spikes and sharp waves (hypsarrhythmia)	
Unilateral Seizures	Partial discharge predominantly over one hemisphere	Usually focal discharge

TABLE 10

Evaluation of Seizures

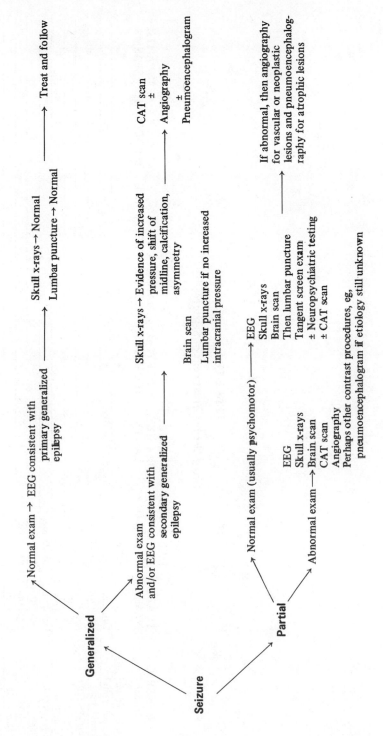

Seizure

Generalized

Partial

Normal exam → EEG consistent with primary generalized epilepsy → Skull x-rays → Normal
Lumbar puncture → Normal → Treat and follow

Abnormal exam and/or EEG consistent with secondary generalized epilepsy → Skull x-rays → Evidence of increased pressure, shift of midline, calcification, asymmetry → CAT scan ± Angiography ± Pneumoencephalogram

Brain scan

Lumbar puncture if no increased intracranial pressure

Normal exam (usually psychomotor) → EEG
Skull x-rays
Brain scan
Then lumbar puncture
Tangent screen exam
± Neuropsychiatric testing
± CAT scan → If abnormal, then angiography for vascular or neoplastic lesions and pneumoencephalography for atrophic lesions

Abnormal exam → EEG
Skull x-rays
Brain scan
CAT scan
Angiography
Perhaps other contrast procedures, eg, pneumoencephalogram if etiology still unknown

13

TABLE 11

Drugs Used in Treatment of Seizures

GENERIC NAME	TRADE NAME	TOTAL DAILY DOSE (per kg body weight)	PARTIAL (ELEMENTARY)	PARTIAL (COMPLEX)	MAJOR MOTOR	PETIT MAL	MYOCLONIC	INFANTILE SPASMS
Diphenylhydantoin	Dilantin	4–7 mg	+	+	+			
Phenobarbital	Luminal	1–5 mg	As added to DPH	+	+			
Primidone	Mysoline	10–25 mg	+	+	+			
Carbamazepine	Tegretol	7–15 mg	+	+	+			
Ethosuximide	Zarontin	20–30 mg				+		
Trimethadione	Tridione	10–25 mg				+		
Paramethadione	Paradione	10–25 mg				+		
Mephenytoin	Mesantoin	7–12 mg	+	+	+			
Ethotoin	Peganone	10–20 mg	+	+	+			
Metharbital	Gemonil	2.5–10 mg	+		+			
Mephobarbital	Mebaral	2.5–10 mg	+		+			
Methsuximide	Celontin	10–20 mg				+		
Phenacemide	Phenurone	25–45 mg	+	+				
Acetazolamide	Diamox	5–15 mg	+			+ and premenstrual		

Drug	Brand	Dosage	Indication	
ACTH		40-60 units total per day		+
Corticosteroids		5-60 mg total per day		+
Diazepam	Valium	0.15-2 mg	+ and status	
Chlordiazepoxide	Librium	1-4 mg	Alcohol withdrawal	
Paraldehyde		0.3-0.7 ml	Alcohol withdrawal	
Dextroamphetamine	Dexedrine	0.2-0.3 mg	Tonic seizures	
Methylphenidate	Ritalin	0.2-0.3 mg	Tonic seizures	+
Clonazepam	Clonapin	0.1-0.2 mg	+	

TABLE 12

Pharmacologic Properties
of Drugs Used in Treatment of Seizures

GENERIC NAME	TRADE NAME	THERAPEUTIC BLOOD LEVEL	AVERAGE HALF-LIFE (hours)	ACTIVE METABOLITE
Diphenylhydan-toin	Dilantin	9–20 µg/ml	24	0
Phenobarbital	Luminal	20–50 µg/ml	96	0
Cabamazepine	Tegretol	2–10 µg/ml	12	0
Primidone	Mysoline	4–14 µg/ml (more accurate to measure phenobarbital level of 20–50 µg/ml, and thus requires 2–3 weeks to stabilize on a given dosage)	12 / 36 / 96	0 / Phenylethylmalon-amide / Phenobarbital
Ethosuximide	Zarontin	45–90 µg/ml	35	0
Trimethadione	Tridione	15–40 µg/ml	16	0
		600-1,000µg/ml (about 20:1 ratio)	>100	Dimethadione

TABLE 13

Treatment of Status Epilepticus (Adult)

1. Prevent aspiration, maintain airway
2. Remove restrictive clothing
3. Start intravenous line—D5NS
4. Take maneuvers to prevent tongue-biting; avoid restraining to point of injury
5. Draw blood for metabolic studies
6. Give thiamine, 100 mg intravenously
7. Give glucose, 50 ml of D50W
8. Give Dilantin, 500 to 1,000 mg intravenously (12-15 mg/kg), at a rate of 50 mg/minute with cardiac monitor
9. If activity persists, either:
    A. Give Valium, 10 mg intravenously (observe for respiratory depression) or
    B. Give phenobarbital, 5–8 mg/kg slowly intravenously, then 4–8 mg/kg intramuscularly every 2–6 hours, not to exceed 1–2 g in 24 hours
10. Alternatively:
    A. Initiate treatment with phenobarbital, 5–8 mg/kg slowly intravenously, then 4 mg/kg intramuscularly or intravenously every 2–6 hours
    B. Paraldehyde, 0.5–0.15 mg/kg orally, per rectum, or intramuscularly (be certain this is deep intramuscular injection), or 0.1 mg/kg slowly intravenously in 50–100 ml solvent, not to exceed 8 ml intravenously
11. Use anesthesia as a last resort

2
Weakness

When a patient presents with weakness, the physician must consider many possible causes. The differential diagnosis is so wide-ranging that an evaluation for all the possible causes of weakness not only would be cumbersome but also would be costly to the patient financially and costly of the physician's time. Perhaps even more important, the patient would be exposed to potentially hazardous and painful tests that might be unnecessary. It is therefore desirable to ascertain the anatomic locus of the patient's weakness. Table 1 provides a guide for making the differential diagnosis between upper and lower motor neuron weakness.

UPPER MOTOR NEURON WEAKNESS

After ascertaining that upper motor neuron weakness is present, then a distinction must be made as to whether the weakness is being caused by hemispheric brainstem or cord dysfunction (Table 2).

Weakness from Hemispheric Disease

The differential diagnosis of a lesion localized to one hemisphere is outlined in Table 3. The patient's history is important in differential diagnosis. Typically, tumors have a slow onset, while vascular disease usually has a stuttering or rapid onset. Occasionally a patient has rapid onset of symptoms from a tumor, but these tumors are usually malignant gliomas (ie, glioblastoma multiforme) or metastatic tumors. The most common type of metastatic tumors to the cerebral hemispheres are those from the lung, breast, kidney, and skin (ie, melanoma). A history of multifocal neurologic disturbances with exacerbations and remissions suggests the diagnosis of a demyelinating disease. Laboratory studies that may be helpful are skull films, EEG, radioisotope scan, or computerized tomography (CT). If a mass lesion is present, arteriography may be required.

Brainstem Weakness

Brainstem lesions that produce weakness are very similar to those that produce hemispheric weakness; therefore the list will not be reiterated. In addition to those listed in Table 3, there are several other diseases, such as syringobulbia and neuroma, that must be considered. Also see Chapter 9, Cranial Nerve Dysfunction.

Myelopathy

If a patient has upper motor neuron weakness of spinal cord origin, the differential diagnosis outlined in Table 5 must be considered. Very often different diseases will affect different portions of the cord. The differential between these diseases can be reduced if one can determine how the cord is being injured. The cord may be injured in at least six distinct ways (Fig. 1): (1) complete transection, (2) hemisection (Brown-Séquard syndrome), (3) posterior columns, (4) corticospinal dysfunction, (5) anterior two-thirds, and (6) core dysfunction. The differential features of these lesions are found in Table 4. The type of lesion produced by the disease and the type of onset are listed in Table 5.

LOWER MOTOR NEURON WEAKNESS

After the clinician has decided that the patient has lower motor neuron disease, he must, if possible, localize the dysfunction to the anterior horn cell, nerve (root or peripheral nerve), myoneural junction, or muscle (see Table 6). Frequently, laboratory studies are needed to help make the differential diagnosis (Table 7).

Motor Neuropathies and Amyotrophies

Although, as indicated in Table 6, most neuropathy is present with sensory symptoms, occasionally one will encounter a patient with motor unit weakness who has minimal or no sensory findings. The diseases that can produce motor neuropathies and amyotrophies are outlined in Table 8.

Diseases of Spinal Roots

The diseases that affect the spinal roots are many; they are listed in Table 9. Typically, any disease that affects the roots may produce the following symptoms: (1) local pain (ie, cervical, thoracic, lumbar); (2) pain to local percussion; (3) radicular pain and paresthesias; (4) increased pain with movement, stretching the root (straight-leg-raising and dorsiflexion of foot), and maneuvers that transiently increase CSF pressure (cough, sneeze); (5) sensory loss in radicular pattern (see Chapter 3, Table 2); (6) muscle spasm (paravertebral muscles); (7) muscle weakness in the distribution of affected roots (Tables 10 and 11); (8) muscle atrophy in distribution of affected roots; (9) decrease or loss of deep tendon reflexes in the distribution of the affected roots.

Neuropathy

When a weak patient presents with evidence of motor unit dissease and the cause is not myopathic, then the patient is probably suffering with a neuropathy. The differential diagnosis of neuropathy includes a great many diseases that present with similar symptoms (ie, symmetric distal sensorimotor loss). Occasionally, however, patients with neuropathy may present with the following symptoms: (1) thickened nerves (hypertrophic neuropathies); (2) mononeuritis (for motor distribution see Table 11; for sensory distribution see Chapter 3, Fig. 3); (3) radiculopathy (for motor distribution see Table 11; for sensory distribution see Chapter 3, Figs. 1 and 2); (4) cranial nerve involvement; (5) autonomic disturbances; (6) ascending neuritis; (7) weakness without sensory findings. The neuropathies presenting in these unique ways are listed in Table 12. A differential diagnosis of all of the major neuropathies can be found in Table 13.

Table 14 is a list of the most common entrapment neuropathies. If the etiology of a neuropathy is not clear, all laboratory studies may be helpful. These are listed in Table 15.

Diseases of the Myoneural Junction

There are three major diseases that affect the myoneural junction (myasthenia gravis, Eaton-Lambert syndrome, and botulism). The differential diagnosis among diseases can be found in Table 16.

Myopathies

After it is determined that weakness is being produced by a defect in the motor unit (ie, neuron, myoneural junction, and muscle) and that the defect is not in the anterior horn cell, root, nerve, or myoneural junction, then the differential diagnosis of myopathies must be considered. There are many diseases that cause muscle dysfunction; however, these can be classified into six major groups: (1) dystrophies, (2) inflammatory diseases (myositis), (3) metabolic diseases, (4) endocrine diseases, (5) toxic myopathies, and (6) congenital diseases. The differential diagnosis among these major categories is listed in Table 17.

The differential diagnosis among the dystrophies is found in Table 18. There is no known treatment that can prevent or reverse the progressive wasting and weakness in these diseases; however, the diagnosis is important because of the genetic and prognostic implications. The myotonia associated with myotonic dystrophy can be treated with quinine, procaine amide, or diphenylhydantoin. Myotonia (continued active contractions of muscles that persist after cessation of effort) can be seen in diseases other than myotonic dystrophy (ie, dyskalemic myopathies, paramyotonia, myotonia congenita), and pseudomyotonia can be seen in hypothyroidism (see Table 21).

Congenital myopathies are rare diseases; unlike dystrophies, they are usually mild, with normal enzymes. These are listed in Table 19.

The differential diagnosis of myositis is given in Table 20, and that of the endocrine myopathies is given in Table 21.

The differential diagnosis of periodic paralysis can be found in Table 22, and that of myoglobinuria in Table 23.

TABLE 1

Differential Diagnosis Between Upper and Lower Motor Neuron Weakness

SIGNS AND SYMPTOMS	UPPER MOTOR NEURON WEAKNESS (UMN)	LOWER MOTOR (NEURON AND MUSCLE) WEAKNESS (LMN)
Weakness distribution	UMN is greater in extensors of upper extremities and flexors of lower extremities (pyramidal distribution) UMN usually involves one side of body, but may also produce paraparesis, quadriparesis or rarely monoparesis UMN usually does not produce weakness in one muscle group or bilateral cranial nerve weakness	Nonpyramidal distribution May present with weakness in one muscle group, paraparesis, quadriparesis, and bilateral cranial nerve weakness
Deep tendon reflexes (DTR's)	In UMN, DTR's are usually increased, but acutely may be decreased; also may be decreased with parietal and cerebellar lesions	Decreased
Tone to passive motion	Increased (see Chap. 4) for differential diagnosis of tone abnormalities; may be decreased with cerebellar and parietal lesions	Decreased
Pathologic reflexes	Present	Absent
Associated symptoms	Defect of cortical association areas (see Chap. 6) Frontal release signs (see Chap. 6) Defect of sensation (see Chap. 3) Cerebellar defects (see Chap. 4) Cranial nerve (see Chap. 9)	Cranial nerve signs (see Chap. 9) Sensory signs (see Chap. 3)

TABLE 2

Differential Diagnosis of Upper Motor Neuron Weakness

SYMPTOM	HEMISPHERIC	BRAINSTEM	CORD
Weakness	(1) Almost always unilateral; (2) usually will affect upper and lower extremities; (3) with midline lesion, there may be bilateral lower-extremity weakness	May be unilateral or bilateral	(1) Usually bilateral; (2) if unilateral, pain and temperature may be decreased in opposite extremity; (3) lower extremities more frequently affected than upper extremities; (4) motor level with increased DTR's below level, absent DTR's at level; (5) may have atrophy at level
Cranial nerve defects (see Chap. 9)	May have: II–hemanopsia; III, IV, VI–eye deviates toward lesion and away from hemiparesis; pupils normal except in carotid disease; V–corneal reflex decrease; VII–lower facial weakness; XI–head deviation toward lesion; X, XII–palate and tongue may deviate transiently	May have: III, IV, VI–nerve paresis; eyes deviate toward hemiparesis; pupil abnormalities; V–motor weakness and decreased sensation; VII–upper and lower face weakness; VIII–vertigo and deafness; IX–decreased sensation and absent gag; difficulty swallowing	None
Sensory defects (see Chap. 3)	May have (1) hemianesthesia (2) disorders of cortical sensation (ie, astereognosis, agraphesthesia, position sense abnormality)	May have (1) hemianesthesia; (2) loss of pain and temperature with intact vibration and position; (3) loss of position and vibration, intact pain and temperature	May have (1) position and vibration absent on one extremity, pain and temperature in other extremity; (2) sensory level on trunk; (3) absence of pain and temperature unilaterally or bilaterally with intact position and vibration; (4) opposite of No. 3; (5) capelike distribution
Bladder dysfunction (see Chap. 7)	Usually absent; may be present with bilateral disease	Usually absent; may be present with bilateral disease	Usually present
Cerebellar defects (see Chap. 4)	Absent	May be present	Absent
Behavior disturbances (see Chap. 6)	Aphasia, agnosia, apraxia, agraphia, alexia, etc	Absent	Absent

22

TABLE 3

Common Diseases That May Produce Hemispheric Weakness in the Adult

TUMORS
Gliomas
　Astrocytoma
　Glioblastoma
　Oligodendroglioma
Meningioma
Ependymoma
Metastatic tumors
Other tumors

DEGENERATIVE DISEASE
Multiple sclerosis

VASCULAR DISEASE (see Chap. 11)
Hemorrhage
　Intracerebral
　　Hypertensive
　　Bleeding disorder
　Subarachnoid
　　Aneurysm
　　Atrioventricular malformation
Thrombosis
　Atherosclerotic
　Collagenosis
　Infectious vasculitis
Embolus
Migraine (see Chap. 1)

TRAUMA
Subdural
Epidural
Intracerebral hematoma
Contusion and laceration

INFECTIOUS AND INFLAMMATORY DISEASE (see Chap. 10)
Abscess
Encephalitis
Meningitis
Syphilis
Fungi and parasites
Sarcoidosis

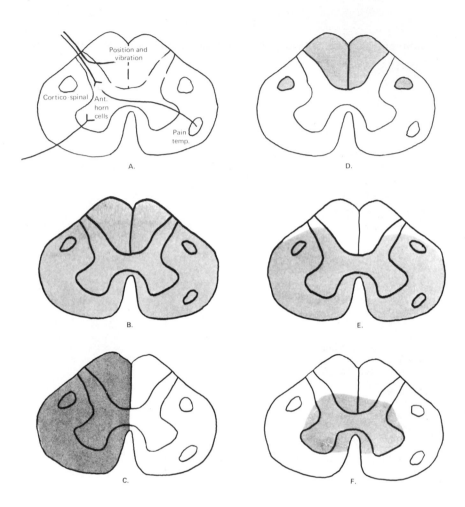

FIG. 1. Pathologic anatomy underlying myelopathy. **A.** Functions of various portions of cord. **B.** Complete transection. **C.** Hemisection. **D.** Posterior columns and corticospinal tract (funicular myelopathy). **E.** Anterior two-thirds. **F.** Core.

TABLE 4

Signs and Symptoms Associated with Various Forms of Myelopathy

FORM	WEAKNESS	SENSATION	DEEP TENDON REFLEXES AND BABINSKI RESPONSE	NEUROGENIC BLADDER
Complete transection	Bilateral weakness	Bilateral loss of all modalities below level of lesion	Below level of lesion, DTR's may be decreased initially (spinal shock), but then bilateral increase with bilateral extensor plantar response	Present (see Chap. 7)
Hemisection	Ipsilateral weakness	Below lesion ipsilateral vibration and position loss, contralateral pain and temperature loss at level of lesion all sensory loss ipsilateral	Increased DTR's and extensor plantar (ipsilateral)	May be absent
Posterior columns	No weakness; often associated with corticospinal tract involvement	Position and vibration loss	Normal (or may be increased or decreased, depending on disease)	May be absent; usually present (see Chap. 7)
Corticospinal	Unilateral or bilateral weakness	No sensory loss	Same as complete transection	Same as cord transection
Anterior two-thirds	Bilateral weakness; upper motor neuron below level of lesion, lower motor neuron at level	Position and vibration spared; may have sacral sparing	Same as complete transection	Same as cord transection
Central core	May have lower motor neuron signs at level; in late stages, upper motor neuron signs	At level of lesion, pain and temperature absent with position and vibration spared; if lesion enlarges, may be loss of sensation with sacral sparing	Early in disease, decreased DTR's at level of lesion without Babinski; late in disease, may look like complete transection	May be absent or present

TABLE 5

Diseases That May Produce Myelopathy

TYPE	ASSOCIATED SYMPTOMS	TYPE OF LESION	NATURE OF ONSET
Tumors			
Intrinsic			
Ependymoma		Hemisection or core	Slow
Glioma		Hemisection or core	Slow
Metastatic	Dysfunction in other parts of body	Hemisection or core	Slow to rapid
Other			
Extrinsic			
Neurofibroma	Radiculopathy	Corticospinal or hemi-section	Slow
Meningioma	Radiculopathy	Corticospinal or hemi-section	Slow
Metastatic	Radiculopathy and back pain	Corticospinal or hemi-section	Slow to rapid
Other			
Trauma			
Fracture displacement	Neck pain and stiffness	Complete transection	Rapid
Hematomyelia	Neck pain and stiff-ness	Core	Rapid
Cervical spondy-losis	Neck pain and stiff-ness	Corticospinal below C-7 level; posterior column	Slow
Cervical disk	Neck pain and stiff-ness with radicular complaints	Complete or hemi-section	Rapid
Odontoid hypo-plasia		Corticospinal	May be slow or cause recurrent problem
Vascular Disease			
Infarction (an-terior spinal artery)	Back pain	Anterior two-thirds	Rapid
Thrombosis			
Vasculitis			
Luetic			
Collagenosis			
Embolus			
Dissecting aortic aneurysm			
Surgery	Usually aortic or sympathectomy		
Hemorrhage			
Malformation ⎱ Bleeding dis- ⎰ order	May have transient symptoms: stiffness, headache, severe back pain	Usually transection	Rapid

TABLE 5 (CONT)

TYPE	ASSOCIATED SYMPTOMS	TYPE OF LESION	NATURE OF ONSET
Infections			
Viral			
Poliomyelitis (acute anterior myelitis)	See Table 8 (this chapter) and Chap. 10	Anterior horn cell	Rapid
Other viruses (ie, coxsackie, echo, arthropod-borne, etc)	Frequently associated with aseptic meningitis and encephalitis (see Chap. 10)	Like polio (see Table 8 and Chap. 10)	Rapid
Bacterial			
Pyogenic abscess Intramedullary	Usually comes from another site; signs of sepsis, tenderness at level of abscess, stiff neck	Core and posterior; may be other types	Rapid
Extramedullary		Transverse and other types; most common below T-4	Rapid to slow
Tuberculoma	May be associated with TB in other parts of body		
Toxins and Physical Agents			
Contrast material	Usually occurs with repeated injections	Anterior two-thirds	Rapid
Spinal anesthesia		In rapid cases transverse myelitis; in slow (arachnoiditis), picture is multifocal	Rapid or chronic
Radiation	Risk increases with survival time, volume of cord irradiated, duration of total dose; frequently Lhermitte's sign is first symptom	Transverse	Slow, with delayed onset 1 month to 5 years after radiation
Electrical injury		Posterior and lateral columns (funicular) with anterior horn cells	Acute to chronic
Deficiency Diseases			
B_{12} subacute combined degeneration	Anemia, neuropathy, dementia, visual change, cerebellar	Posterior columns and lateral column	Chronic
Pellagra	Dermatitis, dementia diarrhea, death		

TABLE 5 (CONT)

TYPE	ASSOCIATED SYMPTOMS	TYPE OF LESION	NATURE OF ONSET
Remote effects of neoplasia	Associated with lymphomas and carcinoma	Patchy lesions most severe in cervical region	Subacute
Degenerative Diseases			
Multiple sclerosis	Multifocal neurologic signs with exacerbations and remissions	Any type	Slow to rapid
Devic's disease	Similar to above	Similar to above; transection	Rapid
Syringomyelia	Scoliosis, sympathetic dysfunction, sensory loss (ie, pain and temperature), muscle atrophy, arthritis, cranial nerve abnormalities	Usually core	Slow
Spinocerebellar	See Chapter 4	Corticospinal, posterior columns	Slow
Familial spastic paraplegia	May be similar to above	Corticospinal	Slow
Amyotrophic lateral sclerosis	Fasciculations, atrophy, weakness, bulbar signs	Anterior horn cell and corticospinal tracts	Slow

TABLE 6

Clinical Differential Diagnosis of Motor Unit Weakness

SIGNS AND SYMPTOMS	NEUROP-ATHY	MYOPATHY	MOTOR NEURON OR ANTERIOR HORN CELL	MYONEURAL JUNCTION
Distribution	(1) Mainly distal or (2) nerve distribution	Mainly proximal	May be distal or proximal and involve midline muscles (eg, neck flexor weakness)	Mainly bulbar, respiratory, and proximal
DTR's	Decreased	Decreased	Frequently increased because of lateral sclerosis	Normal
Myotatic reflux	Increased	Decreased	Increased	Normal
Sensory loss and paresthesias	Usually present (see Chap. 3)	Absent	Absent	Absent
Fasciculation	May be present	Absent	Present	Absent
Atrophy	May be present	May be present	Present	Absent
Fatigue	Mild	Mild	Mild	Severe
Tenderness	May have dysesthesia	May be present	Frequent cramps	
Special characteristics found in specific diseases		Myoglobinuria, myotonia		

TABLE 7

Laboratory Differential Diagnosis of Motor Unit Weakness

TEST	NEUROP-ATHY	MYOPATHY	MOTOR NEURON OR ANTERIOR HORN CELL	MYONEURAL JUNCTION
Enzymes, eg, CPK, aldolase	Normal or mildly elevated	Normal to highly elevated	Normal or slightly elevated	Normal
Nerve conduction	May be slowed	Normal	Usually normal or mildly slowed	Normal
EMG	Fibrillation, fasciculations, giant and polyphasic potentials	Small, low-amplitude potentials	Fibrillations, fasciculations, polyphasic and giant potentials	Electrical fatigue
Muscle biopsy	Grouped atrophy	See Table 17	Grouped atrophy	Normal
Tensilon test	Unchanged, increased fasciculations	Unchanged	Occasionally slight improvement; increased fasciculations	Marked improvement
Lumbar puncture	May have increased protein, pleocytosis	Normal	Normal	Normal
Nerve biopsy	See Table 13	Normal	Normal	Normal

TABLE 8

Motor Neuropathies and Amyotrophies

DISEASE	AGE AT ONSET	SYSTEMIC RELATED SYMPTOMS	MOTOR SIGNS AND SYMPTOMS	SPINAL FLUID	ELECTRICAL STUDIES	OTHER STUDIES
Inflammatory Poliomyelitis	Any age	May have autonomic imbalance, myocarditis, fever, pneumonitis, hypertension	Muscle pains before weakness, which is first in large muscle of proximal joints; is asymmetric; cranial nerves may be involved	Pleocytosis, 10–3,000; increased protein, 30–120	Fibrillation, fasciculation	Viral cultures
Ascending (acute) polyneuritis (Guillain-Barré syndrome)	Any age, especially 20–50 years	May follow febrile illness; may have mild sensory symptoms and radicular pain; may have papilledema, hypertension, arrhythmia, bladder and bowel dysfunction; may have mental symptoms	Usually affects lower extremities before upper; however, may start with cranial nerves symmetrically; takes 10–14 days to reach peak and usually ascends	No pleocytosis (less than 20 cells); protein elevated	May have normal conduction times	May have positive test for mononucleosis, abnormal liver tests
Toxin neuropathy Acute porphyria		May be precipitated by medication (eg, barbiturates, sulfonamides), sun, and alcohol; abdominal pains, mental signs, recurrent attacks	Similar to Guillain-Barré syndrome	Similar to Guillain-Barré syndrome		Increased urinary porphobilinogen

TABLE 8 (CONT)

DISEASE	AGE AT ONSET	SYTEMIC RELATED SYMPTOMS	MOTOR SIGNS AND SYMPTOMS	SPINAL FLUIDS	ELECTRICAL STUDIES	OTHER STUDIES
Lead neuropathy	Children and adults		Not always symmetric; affects upper extremities, especially distal extensor muscles			Lead
Mercury neuropathy		May have ataxia, tremor, and dementia				Mercury
Hereditary degenerative Infantile muscular atrophy (Werdnig-Hoffmann syndrome) (see Chap. 15)	Infancy	Almost always fatal; dysphagia and respiratory insult	Floppy infant (see Chap. 15); retarded motor milestones, absent DTR's, froglike posture; fasciculations not seen in limbs	Normal	Few fasciculations; normal conduction velocity	Normal muscle enzymes

Juvenile muscular atrophy (Wohlfahrt-Kugelberg-Wellander) (see Chap. 15)	Between infancy and adulthood	More benign than infantile muscular atrophy and amyotrophic lateral sclerosis	Mainly proximal limb weakness, legs greater than arms; neck and cranial nerves spared; may have cramps	Normal	Fasciculations, fibrillations; normal conduction	May have slight increase in muscle enzymes
Amyotrophic lateral sclerosis	30–60 years; may be familial	May be associated with diabetes; remote carcinoma; macroglobulinemia and myeloma	All major muscle groups may be involved; may have upper motor neuron signs; cranial nerves frequently involved; frequent severe cramps	Normal	Fasciculations, fibrillations; giant potentials	May have slight increase of muscle enzymes; may have carcinoma, myeloma, etc

TABLE 9

Diseases of Spinal Roots (Radiculopathy)

ETIOLOGY	SYMPTOMS	DIAGNOSTIC STUDIES	TREATMENT
Trauma			
Acute intervertebral disk prolapse	See text, Diseases of Spinal Roots; most common in low cervical and lumbar areas (see Table 10); onset acute	Spine films, myelogram, electrical (EMG) studies	If only pain, treat conservatively (rest, collar, analgesics, muscle relaxants, and heat); if motor loss, consider surgical intervention
Avulsion	Usually severe motor and sensory loss associated with injuries to head and shoulders		Supportive
Tumors			
(neurofibromas or neurinoma, meningioma, lipomas, dermoids, ependymomas of the filum terminal)	Signs are progressive but may be acute; meningiomas occur most commonly in women in thoracic spine; neurofibroma may cause pain with other signs; lipomas, dermoids, and ependymomas of the filum produce the cauda syndrome (see Table 10)	Spine x-rays, myelogram	Surgical intervention
Dysraphism	Frequently associated with cauda syndrome; frequently associated with Arnold-Chiari malformation		Surgery

TABLE 9 (CONT)

Diseases of Spinal Roots (Radiculopathy)

ETIOLOGY	SYMPTOMS	DIAGNOSTIC STUDIES	TREATMENT
Inflammation			
Toxic	Usually occurs during or after myelography or spinal anesthesia and produces arachnoiditis	Myelogram	Removal of agent; ? steroids
Chronic meningitis (TBc, fungi, and pyogenic)	Multiple roots; may also affect cranial nerves and also produce myelopathy	Cultures and antibody titers	Appropriate antibiotic or chemotherapeutic agent
Syphilis			
Tabes dorsalis	Loss of position and vibration; superficial pain and temperature intact; radicular pain; small pupils nonreactive to light; decreased reflexes	VDRL and FTA, LP	Antibiotic
Meningovascular	Similar to chronic meningitis	VDRL and FTA, LP	Antibiotic
Sarcoidosis	May produce uveitis and cranial nerve defects as well as systemic signs	Skin tests, x-rays of chest and bones, serum Ca^{++}, etc; biopsy	Steroids
Neoplastic (carcinomatous meningitis): lung, breast, GI, medulloblastomas	May produce multiple root signs, myelopathy, as well as affecting cranial nerves	Myelogram, LP with cytology, surgical biopsy	Radiation therapy; cytotoxic agents
Idiopathic	Similar to chronic meningitis	All studies negative for etiology	? steroids

TABLE 10

Common Root Syndromes

LOCATION	MOTOR WEAKNESS	SENSORY LOSS	DEEP TENDON REFLEX ABNORMALITIES
S-1 nerve root (disk usually between L-5 and S-1)	Plantar flexion of foot (gastrocnemius and soleus)	Lower posterior calf and lateral portion of foot	Ankle jerk and external hamstring decreased
L-5 nerve root (disk usually between L-4 and L-5)	Peroneal, anterior and posterior tibial and toe extensors	Medial half of foot and lateral calf	Internal hamstring reflex and peroneal reflex decreased
L-4 nerve root (disk usually between L-3 and L-4)	Leg extensors (quadriceps)	Medial calf	Knee jerk decreased
Cauda equina	Flaccid paraplegia, neurogenic bladder, impotence	Perianal	All deep tendon reflexes decreased in lower extremities
C-6 root (disk between C-5 and C-6)	Biceps and brachioradialis (flexion at elbow)	Thumb and index finger	Brachioradialis and biceps slightly decreased
C-7 root (disk between C-6 and C-7)	Triceps and pronator teres (extension at elbow and pronation)	Middle finger	Triceps decreased
C-5 root (disk between C-4 and C-5)	Deltoid and biceps	Lateral aspect of upper arm	None, or biceps decreased

TABLE 11

Segmental Innervation of Muscles and Motor Function Chart*

SHOULDER GIRDLE AND UPPER EXTREMITY

Action to Be Tested	Muscles	Cord Segment	Nerves
Flexion of neck, Extension of neck, Rotation of neck, Lateral bending of neck	Deep neck muscles (sternomastoid and trapezius also participate)	C-1, C-2, C-3, C-4	Cervical
Elevation of upper thorax	Scaleni	C-3, C-4, C-5	Phrenic
Inspiration	Diaphragm		
Adduction of arm from behind to front	Pectoralis major and minor	C-5, C-6, C-7, C-8, T-1	Thoracic anterior (from med. and lat. cords of plexus)
Forward thrust of shoulder	Serratus anterior	C-5, C-6, C-7	Long thoracic
Elevation of scapula	Levator scapulae	C-5, C-3, C-4	Dorsal scapular
Medial adduction and elevation of scapula	Rhomboids	C-4, C-5	Dorsal scapular
Abduction of arm	Supraspinatus	C-4, C-5, C-6	Suprascapular
Lateral rotation of arm	Infraspinatus	C-4, C-5, C-6	

TABLE 11 (CONT)

SHOULDER GIRDLE AND UPPER EXTREMITY (Cont)

Action to Be Tested	Muscles	Cord Segment	Nerves
Medial rotation of arm	Latissimus dorsi, teres major, and subscapularis	C-5, C-6, C-7, C-8	Subscapular (from posterior cord of plexus)
Adduction of arm from front to back			
Abduction of arm	Deltoid	C-5, C-6	Axillary (from posterior cord of plexus)
Lateral rotation of arm	Teres minor	C-4, C-5	
Flexion of forearm	Biceps brachii	C-5, C-6	Musculocutaneous (from lateral cord of plexus)
Supination of forearm			
Adduction of arm	Coracobrachialis	C-5, C-6 C-7	
Flexion of forearm			
Flexion of forearm	Brachialis	C-5, C-6	
Ulnar flexion of hand	Flexor carpi ulnaris	C-7, C-8, T-1	
Flexion of terminal phalanx of { ring finger, little finger }	Flexor digitorum profundus (ulnar portion)	C-7, C-8, T-1	Ulnar (from medial cord of plexus)
Flexion of hand			
Adduction of metacarpal of thumb	Adductor pollicis	C-8, T-1	
Abduction of little finger	Abductor digiti quinti	C-8, T-1	
Opposition of little finger	Opponens digiti quinti	C-7, C-8, T-1	

Action	Muscle	Segmental innervation	Nerve
Flexion of little finger	Flexor digiti quinti brevis	C-7, C-8, T-1	Ulnar (from medial cord of plexus)
Flexion of proximal phalanx, extension of two distal phalanges, adduction and abduction of fingers	Interossei	C-8, T-1	
Pronation of forearm	Pronator teres	C-6, C-7	
Radial flexion of hand	Flexor carpi radialis	C-6, C-7	
Flexion of hand	Palmaris longus	C-7, C-8, T-1	
Flexion of middle phalanx of { index finger, middle finger, ring finger, little finger }	Flexor digitorum sublimis	C-7, C-8, T-1	Median (C-6, C-7 from lateral cord of plexus; C-8, T-1 from medial cord of plexus)
Flexion of hand			
Flexion of terminal phalanx of thumb	Flexor pollicis longus	C-7, C-8, T-1	
Flexion of terminal phalanx { index finger, middle finger }	Flexor digitorum profundus (radial portion)	C-7, C-8, T-1	
Flexion of hand			
Abduction of metacarpal of thumb	Abductor pollicis brevis	C-7, C-8, T-1	
Flexion of proximal phalanx of thumb	Flexor pollicis brevis	C-7, C-8, T-1	
Opposition of metacarpal of thumb	Opponens pollicis	C-8, T-1	
Flexion of proximal phalanx and extension of the two distal phalanges of { index finger, middle finger }	Lumbricals (the two lateral)	C-8, T-1	
{ ring finger, little finger }	Lumbricals (the two medial)	C-8, T-1	Ulnar

TABLE 11 (CONT)

SHOULDER GIRDLE AND UPPER EXTREMITY (Cont)

Action to Be Tested	Muscles	Cord Segment	Nerves
Extension of forearm	Triceps brachii and anconeus	C-6, C-7, C-8	Radial (from posterior cord of plexus)
Flexion of forearm	Brachioradialis	C-5, C-6	
Radial extension of hand	Extensor carpi radialis	C-6, C-7, C-8	
Extension of phalanges of { index finger, middle finger, ring finger, little finger }; Extension of hand	Extensor digitorum communis	C-6, C-7, C-8	
Extension of phalanges of little finger; Extension of hand	Extensor digiti quinti proprius	C-6, C-7, C-8	
Ulnar extension of hand	Extensor carpi ulnarys	C-6, C-7, C-8	
Supination of forearm	Supinator	C-5, C-6, C-7	
Abduction of metacarpal of thumb; Radial extension of hand	Abductor pollicis longus	C-7, C-8	Radial (from posterior cord of plexus)
Extension of thumb; Radial extension of hand	Extensor pollicis brevis and longus	C-7, C-8; C-6, C-7, C-8	
Extension of index finger; Extension of hand	Extensor indicis proprius	C-6, C-7, C-8	

HIP GIRDLE AND LOWER EXTREMITY

Flexion of hip	Iliopsoas	L-1, L-2, L-3	
Flexion of hip (and eversion of thigh)	Sartorius	L-2, L-3	Femoral
Extension of leg	Quadriceps femoris	L-2, L-3, L-4	
Adduction of thigh	Pectineus	L-2, L-3	
	Adductor longus	L-2, L-3	
	Adductor brevis	L-2, L-3, L-4	Obturator
	Adductor magnus	L-3, L-4	
	Gracilis	L-2, L-3, L-4	
Adduction of thigh Lateral rotation of thigh	Obturator externus	L-3, L-4	
Abduction of thigh Medial rotation of thigh	Gluteus medius and minimus	L-4, L-5, S-1	Superior gluteal
Flexion of thigh	Tensor fasciae latae	L-4, L-5	
Lateral rotation of thigh	Piriformis	L-5, S-1	
Abduction of thigh	Gluteus maximus	L-4, L-5, S-1, S-2	Inferior gluteal
Lateral rotation of thigh	Obturator internus	L-5, S-1	
	Gemelli	L-4, L-5, S-1	Muscular branches from sacral plexus
	Quadratus femoris	L-4, L-5, S-1	

TABLE 11 (CONT)

HIP GIRDLE AND LOWER EXTREMITY (Cont)

Action to Be Tested	Muscles	Cord Segment	Nerves
Flexion of leg (assist in extension of thigh)	Biceps femoris	L-4, L-5, S-1, S-2	Sciatic (trunk)
	Semitendinosus	L-4, L-5, S-1	
	Semimembranosus	L-4, L-5, S-1	
Dorsal flexion of foot Supination of foot	Tibialis anterior	L-4, L-5	Deep peroneal
Extension of toes II–V Dorsal flexion of foot	Extensor digitorum longus	L-5, L-5, S-1	
Extension of great toe Dorsal flexion of foot	Extensor hallucis longus	L-4, L-5, S-1	Deep peroneal
Extension of great toe and the three medial toes	Extensor digitorum brevis	L-4, L-5, S-1	

Function	Muscle	Segment	Nerve
Plantar flexion of foot in pronation	Peronei	L-5, S-1	Superficial peroneal
Plantar flexion of foot in supination	Tibialis posterior and triceps surae	L-5, S-1 S-2	Tibial
Plantar flexion of foot in supination	Flexor digitorum longus	L-5, S-1 S-2	
Flexion of terminal phalanx of toes II–V			
Plantar flexion of foot in supination	Flexor hallucis longus	L-5, S-1, S-2	
Flexion of terminal phalanx of great toe			
Flexion of middle phalanx of toes II–V	Flexor digitorum brevis	L-5, S-1	
Flexion of proximal phalanx of great toe	Flexor hallucis brevis	L-5, S-1 S-2	
Spreading and closing of toes	Small muscles of foot	S-1, S-2	
Flexion of proximal phalanx of toes			
Voluntary control of pelvic floor	Perineal and sphincters	S-2, S-3, S-4	Pudendal

*Modified from Chusid, McDonald: Correlative Neuroanatomy and Functional Neurology, 10th ed., pp. 154–156. Courtesy of Lange Medical Publishers.

TABLE 12

Differential Diagnosis of Neuropathy by Major Clinical Signs

HYPERTROPHIC NEUROPATHIES	MONONEURITIS AND MONONEURITIS MULTIPLEX	NEUROPATHIES THAT MAY AFFECT CRANIAL NERVES	NEUROPATHIES ASSOCIATED WITH AUTONOMIC DISTURBANCES	ASCENDING NEUROPATHIES	MOTOR NEUROPATHIES
Leprosy	Diabetes	Sarcoidosis	Diabetes	Guillain-Barré syndrome	Diabetes
Entrapment neuropathies (see Table 14)	Herpes infection	Angiopathic neuropathies	Alcohol and related nutritional neuropathies (see Table 13)	Porphyria	Vasculitis
Charcot-Marie-Tooth disease	Serum sickness	Rheumatoid arthritis	Amyloidosis	Sarcoidosis	Toxins
Dejerine-Sottas disease	Angiopathic neuropathies	Systemic lupus erythematosus	Porphyria	Neoplasm (ie, lymphoma)	Lead
Refsum's disease	Rheumatoid arthritis	Polyarteritis nodosa	Guillain-Barré syndrome	Macroglobulinemia	Gold
Amyloidosis	Polyarteritis nodosa	Temporal arteritis	Riley-Day syndrome		Nitrofurantoin
Hypothyroidism	Systemic lupus erythematosus	Other	Familiar sensory neuropathy (see Chap. 3, Table 1)		Vinca alkaloids
Acromegaly	Other	Diabetes			Guillain-Barré syndrome
	Syphilis	Guillain-Barré syndrome (Fisher's variant)			Other (see Table 8)
	Leprosy	Porphyria			
	Sarcoidosis	Refsum's disease			
	Myeloma	Amyloidosis			
	Tumors	Tangier disease			
	Primary (ie, neurofibroma)	Myeloma			
	Extrinsic (metastatic)	Syphilis			
	Tangier disease	Diphtheria			
	Entrapment neuropathy	Arsenic			
	Trauma	Tumor			
		Intrinsic			
		Extrinsic			

TABLE 13

Differential Diagnosis of Neuropathy by Etiology

ETIOLOGIC CLASSIFICATION	ONSET	CLINICAL SIGNS	NERVE CONDUCTION AND EMG	PATHOLOGY	OTHER LABORATORY TESTS	TREATMENT AND PROGNOSIS
Endocrine and Systemic Neuropathies						
Diabetes	Chronic	Symmetric distal neuropathy (mainly sensory); may be associated with autonomic neuropathy (pupils, vasomotor, gastrointestinal, and genitourinary)	Prolonged sensory and motor conduction times	Segmental demyelination	Abnormal glucose tolerance; LP may show elevated protein	Supportive, good diabetic control
	Acute	Mononeuropathy, mainly motor, also cranial nerves (ie, III) and diabetic amyotrophy (thigh weakness)	Occlusion of vasa nervorum			Frequently shows spontaneous improvement
	Chronic	Radiculopathy (pseudo tabes dorsalis)		Dorsal root and posterior columns		
Acromegaly	Chronic	Carpal tunnel syndrome (see Table 14); occasionally paresthesias in extremities; may have hypertrophic nerves	Slowed conduction over carpal tunnel	Increased endoneural and perineural connective tissue	Growth hormone	May regress with tumor treatment
Hypothyroidism	Chronic	Carpal tunnel syndrome (see Table 14); thickened nerves; hypertrophic nerves	Slowing over carpal tunnel and slowing of motor and sensory nerves	Segmental demyelination; increased glycogen	T-3, T-4 LP; elevated protein	Thyroid hormone
Uremic neuropathy	Chronic; may be fulminant	Incidence increases with duration and severity of renal failure; peripheral symmetric neuropathy	Slowed conduction	Axonal degeneration and segmental demvelination	Blood urea nitrogen	May improve with dialysis; improves with transplantation

TABLE 13 (CONT)

ETIOLOGIC CLASSIFICATION	ONSET	CLINICAL SIGNS	NERVE CONDUCTION AND EMG	PATHOLOGY	OTHER LABORATORY TESTS	TREATMENT AND PROGNOSIS
Hepatic neuropathy	Subacute	Painful sensory neuropathy usually associated with biliary cirrhosis		Intraneural lipid deposits	Abnormal liver function tests	
Nutritional Neuropathies and Alcoholism						
Beriberi	Chronic	Peripheral symmetric; may be associated with cardiac, visual, oculomotor signs, also hoarseness, memory disorder, and ataxia	Slowing	Segmental demyelination; axonal degeneration		Thiamine
Pellagra	Chronic	Peripheral symmetric neuropathy, dermatitis, diarrhea, and dementia				Niacin
Pyridoxine (B$_6$) deficiency	Subacute or chronic	Frequently seen with isoniazid (INH) treatment; a peripheral symmetric neuropathy				Pyridoxine (B$_6$)
B$_{12}$ deficiency	Chronic	May be caused by pernicious anemia, gastric carcinoma, postgastrectomy, celiac disease, fish tapeworm infection; produces peripheral symmetric neuropathy	May have normal conduction; if decreased, it is usually distal; action potential is reduced		B$_{12}$ level; free gastric acid; Schilling test; stool for ova and parasites; GI series	B$_{12}$
Alcoholism	Chronic	Peripheral symmetric neuropathy associated with multiple dietary insufficiency; may have autonomic disturbances (hypotension and hypothermia, decreased esophageal peristalsis and vagal dysfunction)		Axonal degeneration and myelin degeneration; also dorsal root		Good nutrition; abstinence

Infections and Inflammatory Neuropathies

Herpes virus	Acute or subacute	Mononeuropathy, radiculopathy, cranial neuropathy, associated with vesicular eruption; may have postherpetic pain; may also have weakness and atrophy		May be from either zoster or simplex; inflammation; hemorrhage and death of ganglion cells; also may have poliomyelitis inclusion bodies		
Brachial neuritis	Acute	Frequently associated with inoculations or inflammatory disease; may be familial; pain in arm or neck followed by weakness (shoulder); may have numbness in distribution and circumflex nerve; signs may be bilateral	Slowed conduction proximally		Test for mononucleosis; LP may show cells and increased protein	80% improve spontaneously; ? steroids
Acute inflammatory polyradiculopathy (Guillain-Barré syndrome)	Subacute	Prodromal infection (50% of patients) with measles, rubella, varicella, mumps, influenza, mononucleosis, and vaccination; ascending motor signs with minimal sensory signs that increase for 2 weeks, followed by recovery; proximal weakness may be first sign (ie, cranial nerves); may also be autonomic involvement (sphincter, arrhythmias, bladder, hypotension and hypertension—loss of thermal regulation—also muscle pains); may be recurrent or chronic	Usually conduction slow; however, may have normal conduction	Mononuclear infiltrates and segmental demyelination	LP–elevated protein; no cells; mono test, viral antibodies	Supportive; respiratory failure common cause of death; ? steroids

TABLE 13 (CONT)

ETIOLOGIC CLASSIFICATION	ONSET	CLINICAL SIGNS	NERVE CONDUCTION AND EMG	PATHOLOGY	OTHER LABORATORY TESTS	TREATMENT AND PROGNOSIS
Rheumatoid arthritis	Distal symmetric chronic / Mononeuritis, acute	Most often a mild disease; symmetric sensory neuropathy; as it becomes more severe, it may involve motor nerves; may also demonstrate mononeuritis or mononeuritis multiplex; may involve cranial nerves		Vasculitis and demyelination	Erythrocyte sedimentation rate; rheumatoid factor, etc; complement	Steroids for severe neuropathy / With mononeuritis multiplex, poor prognosis
Polyarteritis nodosa	Similar to above	Both peripheral distal symmetric and mononeuritis multiplex similar to rheumatoid arthritis; also may involve cranial nerves; similar picture may be seen from serum sickness, drug use (ie, amphetamines)		Vasculitis	May have Australia antigen; muscle biopsy	Corticosteroids
Systemic lupus erythematosus		Peripheral symmetric neuropathy, mononeuritis multiplex, proximal weakness with decreased vibration and position		Vasculitis	LP may show elevated protein	Corticosteroids
Scleroderma	Chronic	Peripheral symmetric neuropathy, involves cranial nerves (V)		Vasculitis		
Sjögren's syndrome	Chronic	Similar to above		Vasculitis		
Cranial arteritis	Chronic to acute	Peripheral symmetric or mononeuropathy multiplex		Vasculitis		

Disease	Course	Clinical features	Pathology	Diagnostic	Treatment
Wegener's granulomatosis		Similar to cranial arteritis	Vasculitis		
Leprosy	Chronic to acute	Prior to sensory loss there is local paresthesia; nerves become thickened and painful and become entrapped; since neuropathy is intracutaneous, it does not follow root or nerve distribution in tuberculoid leprosy the sensory loss is in local lesion; if there is nerve trunk near, there may be sensory loss in nerve distribution; in lepromatous leprosy the sensory loss is not confined to the skin lesion, but is usually symmetric and in cold portions of the body (ears, legs, arms); there may be motor involvement late in the disease; includes cranial nerves (ie, VII)	Acid-fast rod (*Mycobacterium leprae*) granulomas (in tuberculoid); in lepromatous, structure of nerve remains, but there is infiltration with bacilli and histiocytes		Sulfone drugs
Sarcoidosis	Acute, but may be subacute or chronic	Cranial nerve defects prominent (ie, VII nerve); may also have ascending neuropathy similar to Guillain-Barré syndrome or peripheral symmetric neuropathy; may also have mononeuritis or radiculopathy	Granuloma	Chest x-ray shows hilar enlargement, anergy; muscle and liver biopsy; Kveim test	Corticosteroids
Diphtheritic neuropathy	Acute or subacute	Cranial nerve (soft palate) followed (8–12 weeks) by peripheral symmetric neuropathy	Segmental demyelination	Slowed conduction	Antitoxin; survives, prognosis is excellent for functional recovery

49

TABLE 13 (CONT)

ETIOLOGIC CLASSIFICATION	ONSET	CLINICAL SIGNS	NERVE CONDUCTION AND EMG	PATHOLOGY	OTHER LABORATORY TESTS	TREATMENT AND PROGNOSIS
Toxic Neuropathies						
Industrial Agents						
Acrylamide		Peripheral symmetric		Axonal degeneration		Removal of toxin; recovery after months
Tri-o-cresyl phosphate		Peripheral symmetric		Axonal degeneration		Removal of toxin; recovery poor
Carbon disulfide		Peripheral symmetric		Axonal degeneration		Recovery poor
Trichloroethylene		Cranial nerve (ie, V)				
N-hexane		Peripheral symmetric		Axonal degeneration		Removal of toxin; improves 1–2 years
Carbon monoxide		Peripheral symmetric		Demyelination		
Polychlorinated biphenyls		Peripheral symmetric				
Metals						
Arsenic		Peripheral symmetric; may involve cranial nerves		Anterior horn cell plus segmental demyelination	Arsenic can be found in hair and urine	? BAL; ? penicillamine: slow improvement

Agent	Onset	Clinical features	Pathology	Diagnosis	Treatment/Course
Lead	Subacute	Upper limbs more involved than lower limbs, especially wrist extensors (radial nerve); sensory signs usually minor; motor signs not always symmetric	Anterior horn cell; segmental demyelination and axonal degeneration	Hair, nails, and urine for lead	Penicillamine
Mercury	Subacute	Peripheral symmetric; may be associated with fasciculations, atrophy, and tremor	Anterior horn cell and nerve demyelination	Hair, nails, and urine for mercury	Penicillamine
Thallium	Subacute	Mainly a sensory neuropathy; may be associated with ataxia, convulsions, retrobulbar neuritis, and baldness	Intraaxonal vacuoles		? hemodialysis and ? potassium; ? dithizon
Drugs					
Chloramphenicol	Chronic	Mild peripheral sensory loss occasionally associated with optic neuritis			
Diphenylhydantoin		Loss of reflexes with mild sensory disturbances			Both recover after drug stopped
Disulfiram		Mainly a peripheral sensory neuropathy			Recovery slow after stopping medicine ? BAL
Gold	Acute	Weakness that may be asymmetric; may involve cranial nerves (VII); may also have sensory symptoms	Axonal degeneration		
Isoniazid		Peripheral symmetric neuropathy (sensorimotor)	Axonal degeneration		Prevention with pyridoxine (B_6)
Nitrofurantoin	Subacute	Peripheral symmetric neuropathy, occasionally may be pure motor	Axonal degeneration		
Vinca alkaloids	Subacute	Peripheral symmetric neuropathy; mild sensory findings with profound motor defect	Axonal degeneration		Recovery following withdrawal of medicine

TABLE 13 (CONT)

Neoplastic Neuropathies

ETIOLOGIC CLASSIFICATION	ONSET	CLINICAL SIGNS	NERVE CONDUCTION AND EMG	PATHOLOGY	OTHER LABORATORY TESTS	TREATMENT AND PROGNOSIS
Carcinomatous neuropathy	Acute to chronic	Peripheral symmetric mainly sensory, but may be sensorimotor; symptoms may precede tumor		Loss of dorsal root fibers; axonal degeneration and demyelination	LP may show elevated protein	Treat underlying neoplasia; however, this frequently does not reverse neuropathy
Lymphomas and leukemia	Acute to chronic	May develop peripheral sensory neuropathy, acute ascending neuropathy similar to Guillain-Barré syndrome; may involve cranial nerves		May have infiltration, dorsal root degeneration, segmental demyelination		May regress with treatment of tumor
Polycythemia		Mainly paresthesia; however, may develop peripheral sensorimotor neuropathy				Treatment of polycythemia arrests neuropathy
Myeloma	Subacute to chronic	Neuropathy may be first signs of disease; peripheral sensorimotor; cranial nerves may be involved; may be severe and cause quadriplegia; may have a mononeuropathy or radiculopathy with plasmacytoma		May have demyelination, degeneration, infiltration; occasionally amyloid		Chemotherapy
Macroglobulinemia		Peripheral symmetric neuropathy; may have ascending neuropathy; may involve cranial nerves		Infiltration occasionally amyloid; also axonal degeneration and demyelination		Chemotherapy

Disease	Course	Clinical Features	Pathology/Lab	Treatment
Cryoglobulinemia		Associated with Raynaud's phenomenon; purpuric skin eruptions; main symptoms are pain and paresthesias; frequently asymmetric		Avoid cold
Local tumors (neurofibromas, schwannoma, metastatic tumors)		Mononeuropathy, mononeuropathy multiplex, radiculopathy, cranial nerves		Surgery

Hereditary Neuropathies

Disease	Course	Clinical Features	Pathology/Lab	Treatment
Refsum's disease	Chronic	Autosomal recessive, retinitis pigmentosa, ataxia, and peripheral symmetric neuropathy; may involve cranial nerves	Hypertrophic nerves with nerves embedded in mucoid matrix; onion bulb formations; LP—elevated protein; phytanic acid elevated	Diet
Leukodystrophies (see Chap. 14)		Usually mental deterioration is the major symptom; however, these patients may have neuropathy	See Chap. 14; See Chap. 14	See Chap. 14
Fabry's disease	Chronic	Intense burning in feet associated with rash; carried by sex-linked recessive genes	Proteinuria and uremia; decreased galactosidase	Dilantin may decrease burning; dialysis and transplantation
Tangier disease	Chronic	Large yellow tonsils, with hepatosplenomegaly; neuropathy that is like mononeuritis multiplex; may involve cranial nerves	Schwann cells with vacuoles and histiocytes	

TABLE 13 (CONT)

ETIOLOGIC CLASSIFICA-TION	ONSET	CLINICAL SIGNS	NERVE CON-DUCTION AND EMG	PATHOLOGY	OTHER LABORATORY TESTS	TREATMENT AND PROGNOSIS
Abetalipo-proteinemia (Bassen-Kornzweig syndrome)	Chronic	Mental retardation, symmetric sensorimotor neuropathy, ataxia, and many other symptoms		Demyelination and axonal degeneration	Acanthocytes; low cholesterol	
Porphyria	Subacute	Abdominal pains, psychologic abnormalities; weakness (can start in upper limbs) symmetric, progressive (1 to 4 weeks); may have sensory defect; cranial nerves may be involved; may have urinary retention and tachycardia and hypertension		Demyelination	Urinary porphyrins	Supportive, stop barbiturates; give glucose, pyridoxine (B_6), hematin

Amyloid (primary and secondary)		Nerves enlarged, autonomic symptoms (bladder and bowel, orthostatic hypotension); may have involvement of cranial nerves; may have entrapment (carpal tunnel syndrome), mononeuropathy, or peripheral symmetric neuropathy	Amyloid deposits in epineural, vascular, and neural tissue; both demyelination and axonal degeneration	EKG abnormalities; proteinuria; liver function abnormality; positive congo red test	Supportive
Charcot-Marie-Tooth disease	Chronic	Autosomal dominant; muscle loss in anterior compartment of legs with footdrop; stork legs; mild sensory loss	Degeneration of axon and myelin		Supportive
Dejerine-Sottas disease	Chronic	Autosomal dominant; may have an intermittent course; hypertropic nerves with peripheral symmetric weakness, atrophy, and sensory loss	Hypertrophy of nerves (especially in limbs), because of marked proliferation of Schwann cells		? steroids ? thiamine

TABLE 14

Compression and Entrapment Neuropathies

NERVE AND SYNDROME	SYMPTOMS	LABORATORY STUDIES AND TREATMENT
Median		Nerve conduction essential in diagnosis of most of the entrapment syndromes
Pronator teres syndrome	Pain in forearm that radiates up or down; repeating gripping or pronation increases pain; numbness and tingling in palm and first 3 fingers	1. Avoid exertion of forearm muscle 2. Surgical decompression
Carpal tunnel syndrome	Pain and paresthesia in hand and wrist, especially during sleep; symptoms increased by wrist and finger flexion; poor co-ordination of finger, and thenar wasting; weakness of opponens pollicis and abductor pollicis brevis; sensory impairment in palm and first 3 fingers; Tinel's sign (shocklike pain with percussion at wrist)	1. May be associated with hypothyroidism, rheumatoid arthritis, pregnancy, acromegaly, myeloma, diabetes; therefore underlying disease should be treated 2. Splinting and local steroids? 3. Surgical decompression
Ulnar Elbow and cubital tunnel	Numbness and tingling in 4 and 5 fingers, clumsiness, atrophy of interossei and weakness of ulnar innervated muscle (see Table 11)	1. Avoid pressure on elbow 2. Surgical transposition
Hand	1. Terminal motor branch produces weakness of interossei, ulnar lumbricals, and adductor pollicis; sensory and hypothenar muscles are normal. 2. Proximal motor branch produces weakness of all ulnar muscles of hand, no sensory loss 3. Compression of nerve as it enters hand affects all ulnar hand muscles and produces decreased sensation in distal ulnar palm and volar surface and 4 and 5 fingers	Since most of these are produced by trauma, trauma should be avoided; occasionally, local tumors, malformations, fractures may also produce picture

Nerve	Clinical features	Management
Radial		
Sleep paralysis or Saturday night palsy	Nerve in arm is compressed against humerus; spares nerve to triceps; otherwise affects all motor (see Table 11) and sensory branches	Avoid pressure; treat fracture
Compression at supinator	Compression at supinator produces weakness in muscles supplied by posterior interosseous branch of radial (cannot straighten fingers, supinate wrist); no sensory impairment; brachioradialis and extensor carpi radialis longus may be spared; if lesion is distal to supinator, this muscle will be spared	Produced by repeated supination or by compression by tumors, fractures, or subluxations
Cutaneous branch	Terminal cutaneous branch produces pain and sensory loss mainly between thumb and index finger	Seen after fracture or with tight bracelets or rope
Lateral femoral cutaneous nerve (meralgia paresthetica)	Burning and sensory loss outer thigh; made worse by standing; improves with sitting or lying prone	Associated with obesity, pregnancy, and diabetes; underlying disease should be treated; abdominal muscles should be strengthened; local steroid injections
Femoral nerve	Weakness and sensory decrease in femoral distribution (see Table 11 and Chap. 3, Fig. 3)	May be associated with inguinal hernia or repair, local tumor, hematoma
Obturator	Weakness and sensory loss in obturator distribution	May be seen with obturator hernia, injury during difficult labor from fetal head or forceps
Ilioinguinal	Pain in groin increased by tension of abdominal wall; sensory loss (see Chap. 3, Fig. 3) and bulging of inguinal region with increased intraabdominal pressure; tenderness medial to anterior superior spine	Local steroids; support; surgical decompression
Peroneal and tibial nerves		
Common peroneal	Occurs mainly at fibular head because of leg-crossing, casts, boots, etc; produces impaired dorsiflexion of toes (footdrop) and impaired eversion (impaired sensation) (see Chap. 3, Fig. 3)	Avoid trauma; decompression
Deep peroneal	Dorsiflexion impaired, eversion spared; sensory loss limited to small area between toes	Decompression

TABLE 14 (CONT)

NERVE AND SYNDROME	SYMPTOMS	LABORATORY STUDIES AND TREATMENT
Superficial peroneal	Weakness of evertors and sensory loss over dorsolateral foot; may also be associated with severe pain	Surgical decompression; local steroids?
Posterior tibial	Pain, paresthesias in sole of foot, increased by standing and walking; does not involve heel; weakness of flexors of toes, and pain with digital pressure applied below medial malleolus	Treat tenosynovitis and arthritis if present; use proper foot support (ie, decrease valgus position of heel); surgical decompression
Plantar nerves	Pain and paresthesia in sole of foot with weakness of intrinsic foot muscle caused by prolonged standing on ladder or high arch supports; tenderness over area of entrapment (medial longitudinal arch near anterior portion of calcaneous)	Local steroids; avoidance of posture; surgical decompression
Interdigital nerves	Produced by hyperextension at the metatarsophalangeal joint in foot; produces pain most frequently between 3 and 4 toes (Morton's neuroma); anesthesia of tips of toes; tenderness of nerve as it crosses deep transverse ligament	Treat arthritis if present; avoid abnormal posture; local steroids; metatarsal bar and support of median longitudinal arch; surgical decompression
Suprascapular nerve	Pain in lateral and posterior shoulder increased by shoulder motion; weakness and atrophy of supraspinatus and intraspinatus muscles; pain with pressure at suprascapular notch and with cross-body adduction of arm	Frequently associated with tenosynovitis, calcium; treat with local steroids and surgical decompression
Dorsal scapular nerve	Pain at medial border of scapula; increased by head rotation or lateral flexion; winging of scapula and tenderness of rhomboids and scalene muscle	Cervical collar or cervical traction; surgical decompression

TABLE 15

Laboratory Studies in Neuropathy

Laboratory studies helpful in evaluating a patient with a neuropathy of unknown etiology are as follows:

Glucose tolerance test
Growth hormone
Thyroid function tests
Blood urea nitrogen
Liver function tests, Australia antigen
B_{12}, free gastric acid, Schilling's test
Viral antibodies, test for mononucleosis
Erythrocyte sedimentation rate, antinuclear antibodies
Rheumatoid factor
Complement
Porphyrins (urine)
Lumbar puncture
Heavy metals (urine, hair, and nails)
Stool guaiacs, gastrointestinal radiologic procedures, x-ray
    of chest
Hematologic studies
Bone marrow
Serum electrophoresis, Bence Jones protein
Nerve biopsy
Muscle biopsy
Electromyography and nerve conduction studies

TABLE 16

Differential Diagnosis of Diseases Affecting the Myoneural Junction

CHARACTERISTICS	MYASTHENIA GRAVIS	CARCINOMATOUS MYOPATHY (Eaton-Lambert Syndrome)	BOTULISM
Etiology	Autoimmune	Unknown	*Clostridium botulinum* toxin
Age and sex	Young females more than males	Older patients, males more than females	No predilection
Associated diseases	Pernicious anemia, thyroid disease, thymoma, systemic lupus erythematosus	Carcinoma of the lung (oat cell) and other neoplastic diseases	Gastrointestinal symptoms
Distribution of weakness	Bulbar muscle, respirations, proximal arm	Mainly limb muscles, associated with aching	Bulbar muscles; respiratory
Repeated exercise	Progressive weakness	Improves	
Reflexes	Normal	Decreased	
EMG	Demonstrates fatigue with repeated stimulation	Demonstrates improvement with rapid repeated stimulation	Slight increase with rapid repeated stimulation
Tensilon test	Positive	Mild improvement	No improvement
Treatment	Thymectomy; neostigmine and pyridostigmine; steroids	Guanidine	Guanidine as Eaton-Lambert syndrome; polyvalent botulinum antitoxin; gastric lavage and cathartics

TABLE 17

Differential Diagnosis of Major Etiologies of Muscle Disease

CHARACTERISTICS	DYSTROPHIES	INFLAMMATORY DISEASES	METABOLIC DISEASES	ENDOCRINE DISEASES	TOXIC MYOPATHIES	CONGENITAL DISEASES
Familial	Yes	No	Yes	No	No	Yes
Pathology (muscle biopsy)	Muscle replaced with fat and connective tissue; central nuclei; necrosis and phagocytosis	Necrotic muscle with cellular exudate, muscle degeneration	Generally not very remarkable in periodic paralysis; in glycogen storage there are enzymatic abnormalities	Usually normal		May show various pathologic defects
Enzymes	Elevated	Elevated	Normal	Normal	Elevated or normal	Normal
Age at onset	Early to late	Late	Early	Usually late	Late	Usually early
Other laboratory tests	Normal	Erythrocyte sedimentation rate; antinuclear antibodies	Serum K^+	T_4, T_3, Ca^{++}, alkaline phosphatase, growth hormone, cortisol		
EMG	Myotonia with myotonic dystrophy	Fibrillations	Myotonia with periodic paralysis	None specific		
Associated signs or symptoms	Mental retardation, cardiac abnormalities, cataracts, frontal balding, gonadal atrophy	Arthritis, Raynaud's phenomenon, malignancies, muscle tenderness, muscle calcification, fever, chills, occasionally ulceration over prominent bones, skin rashes		Systemic signs of endocrine malfunction (eg, myxedema, thyrotoxicosis, etc)		

TABLE 18

Differential Diagnosis of Dystrophy

NAME	INHERITANCE	ONSET	PROGNOSIS	DISTRIBUTION OF WEAKNESS	PSEUDOHYPERTROPHY	ASSOCIATED SIGNS	PATHOLOGY
Duchenne's (severe sex-linked) pseudohypertrophic dystrophy	Sex-linked recessive with 30% mutation rate	First 3 years of life	Rapidly progressive; wheelchair age 8–14 years; death at 10 to 40 years	Proximal greater than distal, pelvic girdle greater than shoulder	May be present leg and calf muscles	EKG abnormalities with arrhythmias; mental abnormality	Fat and collagen replacement of muscle tissue with necrosis and phagocytosis
Becker's (benign sex-linked) dystrophy	X-linked recessive, as above	Later onset than Duchenne's dystrophy	Slower progression than Duchenne's dystrophy	As above	As above		As above
Landouzy-Dejerine (facioscapulohumeral) dystrophy	Autosomal dominant	Usually ages 7–25 years	Slow; normal life span	Face (perioral), scapula, and arm	Uncommon	Cardiac complication rare	As above
Erb's (limb girdle) dystrophy	Autosomal recessive	Age 10–30 years	Varies greatly	Pelvic and shoulder girdle	Common	Cardiac involvement rare	As above

Myotonic dystrophy	Autosomal dominant	Infancy to early adulthood	Progressive; death not uncommon at 40 to 60 years	Starts with facial, distal myotonia and becomes generalized	Absent	Cardiac arrhythmias, frontal baldness, cataracts, retinal abnormalities, small sella and skull abnormalities, mental deficiency, testicular atrophy and smooth muscle dysfunction, low basal metabolic rate, glucose intolerance and abnormal IgG	Rows of central nuclei, sarcoplasmic masses, ring fibers, type I fiber atrophy (eg, high content of oxidative enzymes)
Welander's (distal muscular) dystrophy	Dominant, ? autosomal (men more than women)	Between 20 and 60 years	Very slow	Distal symmetric	May be present	None	Similar to Erb's dystrophy
Kiloh-Nevin's ocular dystrophy	Dominant		Good for life	Mainly eyes and lips; may also involve face and neck; may also appear in limbs; occasionally pharyngeal muscles	None	May be associated with hereditary ataxias and pigmentary retinal degeneration	Ragged red fibers

TABLE 19

Differential Diagnosis of Benign Congenital Myopathies

TYPE OF MYOPATHY	CLINICAL FEATURES	PATHOLOGIC FEATURES
Central core	In addition to proximal weakness, may have shoulder atrophy, clubfoot, congenital hip dislocation	Central cores (dense myofilaments) in type I fibers
Nemaline	Atrophy, proximal weakness including face; may be progressive and may even cause death	Small round rods in muscle fibers
Mitochondrial, megaconial, pleoconial	Proximal weakness, benign	Abnormalities of mitochondria (either enlarged or too many)
Myotubular	May have ophthalmoplegia, facial weakness, footdrop; may be progressive	Long chains of central nuclei
Multicore	Certain features resemble Marfan's syndrome	Multifocal myofibrillar degeneration; decrease of mitochondrial oxidative enzyme activities
Reducing body	Progressive; may lead to death; bilateral ptosis	Bodies with reducing properties in muscle fibers
Fingerprint	Mild disease	Inclusions with concentric lamellae
Type I fiber lysis	Mild; however, enzymes may be elevated	Type I fiber atrophy and fragmented myofibrils

TABLE 20

Differential Diagnosis of Myositis

TYPE	PREDOMINANT SEX AND AGE AT ONSET	UNDERLYING DISEASES	LABORATORY STUDIES	TREATMENT	ASSOCIATED SYMPTOMS
Polymyositis (adult)	Adult female	Diverse etiologies: systemic lupus erythematosus, progressive systemic sclerosis, rheumatoid arthritis, Sjögren's syndrome, giant cell arteritis; most commonly idiopathic, rarely remote effect of tumor	Muscle biopsy demonstrates inflammation and necrosis, enzymes elevated; erythrocyte sedimentation rate elevated; EMG demonstrates myopathic pattern with evidence of hyperexcitability; depending on the underlying disease, other tests may be abnormal	Steroids	Other than weakness (proximal), if patient has associated symptoms, these are related to underlying disease
Dermatomyositis (adult)	Adult female	Frequently associated with Raynaud's phenomenon and scleroderma	Same as above	Steroids	Rash over face in butterfly distribution, dusky red patches over bony prominences; linear hyperemic streaks; also scleroderma
Dermatomyositis (with malignancy)	Adult (both)	10–50% of patients with dermatomyositis older than age 40 have underlying malignancies; most common tumors are lung, breast, and stomach	Same as above	Treatment of underlying malignancy	Same as above

TABLE 20 (CONT)

TYPE	PREDOMINANT SEX AND AGE AT ONSET	UNDERLYING DISEASES	LABORATORY STUDIES	TREATMENT	ASSOCIATED SYMPTOMS
Dermatomyositis (childhood)	Child	May have arthritis; seldom associated with malignancy	Same as above	Usually self-limited disease; steroids may be of help	Same as above; muscles may calcify
Acute myositis (viral polymyositis)	Adult or child	Influenza; picornavirus and myxoviruses	May be associated with abnormal serum viral titers; may have myoglobinuria	Supportive (see myoglobinuria)	
Infectious myositis	Adult or child	Trichinosis; toxoplasmosis (acquired)	*Trichina:* may be encysted, and there may be eosinophilic infiltrate in muscle; embryo may be seen in blood; *Toxoplasma:* pseudocysts do not have inflammatory reaction; positive serologic reaction	Trichinosis: symptomatic; patient may show symptomatic improvement with steroids; toxoplasmosis: sulfonamides and pyrimethamines	Trichinosis: GI symptoms and myalgias; meningitis with cerebral signs may be seen; toxoplasmosis: adenopathy, rash, myocarditis, and meningitis

TABLE 21
Differential Diagnosis of Endocrine Myopathies

TYPE	WEAKNESS	WASTING	OTHER NEUROLOGIC SIGNS AND SYMPTOMS	LABORATORY
Thyrotoxic (hyperthyroidism)	Mainly proximal lower extremities, then proximal upper extremities	Also proximal	DTR's are intact; may be associated with both periodic paralysis and myasthenia gravis	T_4, T_3, RAI, etc
Myxedema (hypothyroidism)	Mainly proximal	May have hypertrophy	Cramps and pain in muscles; DTR's have slow return; pseudomyotonia and myoedema may be present	Same as above
Hyperparathyroidism	Similar to thyrotoxic	Proximal muscles	DTR's may be decreased; muscle hypotonia; frequent mental symptoms	Elevated calcium; elevated alkaline phosphatase; osteomalacia
Acromegaly	Increased strength; however, may lead to hypopituitarism (see below)	Hypertrophy in early stages	See hypopituitarism	Increase growth hormone
Hypopituitarism	Proximal weakness	Wasting	If suprasellar tumor develops, may have visual and hypothalamic signs	Decrease in tropic and end-organ hormone
Cushing's syndrome	Proximal weakness, mainly pelvic girdle; weakness may not improve with treatment; may get worse	No wasting	Mental changes	Plasma cortisol
Steroid myopathy	Similar to above except gets better with stopping medication	May get necrosis	Mental changes	
Addison's disease	Generalized weakness probably related to electrolyte disturbances	Occasional contractures		Plasma cortisol

TABLE 22

Differential Diagnosis of Periodic Paralysis

SYMPTOMS AND SIGNS	HYPOKALEMIA	ADYNAMIA EPISODICA HEREDITARIA (HYPERKALEMIA)	NORMOKALEMIA
Inheritance	Autosomal dominant	Autosomal dominant	Autosomal dominant
Sex	Males more frequently affected than females	Males and females equally affected	Males and females equally affected
Onset	2nd decade	Infancy and childhood (1st decade)	1st decade
Duration	6 hours to 30 days	1 minute to 3 hours	Days to weeks
Weakness	Proximal > distal; lower limbs > arms > neck and face; respiration and swallowing usually not affected; may develop permanent weakness	Myotonia and paramyotonia may be associated with this disease; weakness, trunk > proximal > distal limb; lower extremity > upper; weakness can be decreased with exercise and eating; may also develop permanent weakness	More severe than in hypokalemia and hyperkalemia
Precipitating events	Rest after exercise, heavy meal, anxiety, comes on early morning or in sleep; glucose and insulin; NaCl	Rest after exercise, cold, emotion, infection, KCl	Rest after exercise, alcohol, cold, KCl
Associated symptoms	Bradycardia, EKG abnormal, oliguria, migraine		Salt craving, tachycardia
Laboratory	Hypokalemia	Hyperkalemia	Normokalemia
Treatment	KCl—acute attack; acetazolamide prophylaxis	Calcium gluconate and/or thiazide; acetazolamide prophylaxis	Acetazolamide prophylaxis

TABLE 23
Differential Diagnosis of Myoglobinuria

TYPE	ASSOCIATED SIGNS AND LABORATORY STUDIES
Metabolic	
Glycogen storage disease	
McArdle's disease (phosphorylase deficiency)	Muscle biopsy and enzymatic stains
Tauri disease (phosphofructokinase deficiency)	
Excess lactate production	During exercise lactic acid increases excessively
Impaired fatty acid production	Associated with cramps and impaired fatty acid production
Other (diabetic acidosis, hypothermia, hypokalemia)	May be associated with hyperthermia and rigidity
Toxic	
Alcoholism	May have abnormal ischemic arm test and decreased phosphorylase
Malayan sea snake poisoning	
Drugs (clofibrate, succinylcholine, amphotericin B)	
Inflammatory: acute myositis or myolysis	Biopsy reveals inflammatory changes
Muscle Ischemia and Infarction	
Vascular occlusion secondary to thrombosis and emboli	Arteriography
Pressure	
Crush injury	
Prolonged coma	
Anterior tibial syndrome	
Other exertional syndrome (eg, squat, jump, march, seizures, etc)	

3
Sensory Defects

Patients with sensory defects frequently have associated weakness; therefore the differential diagnosis of sensory defects is very similar to that of weakness. Occasionally, however, a patient may have a sensory defect with a normal motor examination. The nature and distribution of the sensory defect will help localize the defect into one of the following major areas:

1. Cortical: Cortical sensory defects are usually produced by lesions in the parietal lobe, especially the postcentral gyrus. Usually primary (elemental) sensation is spared (pain, temperature, touch, vibration). When one of these patients is stimulated on the contra-lesional side, he can feel the stimulus, but it may have abnormal qualities to it. When executive sensation (ie, stereognosis, graph-esthesia, position sense, two-point discrimination, tactile localiza-tion) is tested, there is a defect on the side contralateral to the lesion. The etiology for these sensory defects is the same as for those that can cause hemispheric weakness (see Chap. 2, Table 3).
2. Subcortical hemispheric lesions: Subcortical lesions may present with symptoms like those of cortical lesions; however, lesions in the thalamus (VPL or VPM) may produce elemental as well as executive sensory defects. These can produce a hemisensory loss not unlike that seen in hysteria. Unlike hysterics, however, who

are indifferent to their loss, these patients have painful dys-esthesias that can be made worse by repeated stimulation to the affected side. The most common etiology is vascular disease; how-ever, tumors can also produce a thalamic sensory syndrome.

3. Brainstem: Brainstem lesions may produce dissociated sensory defects. These sensory defects can be unilateral or bilateral and may involve cranial nerve sensation (see Fig. 4).

4. Cord: The sensory defects seen in cord disease are reviewed in Chapter 2. It is important to remember that the sensory level may be below the level of the lesion.

5. Root: The sensory losses seen in root lesions are illustrated in Figures 2 and 3. See Chapter 2 for etiologies of root disease.

6. Nerve: The distribution of sensory loss seen with nerve lesions can be found in Figure 4.

7. Insensitivity to pain: There are patients who do not perceive pain. Frequently these patients injure themselves and may not have evidence of motor dysfunction. A differential diagnosis of these diseases is found in Table 1.

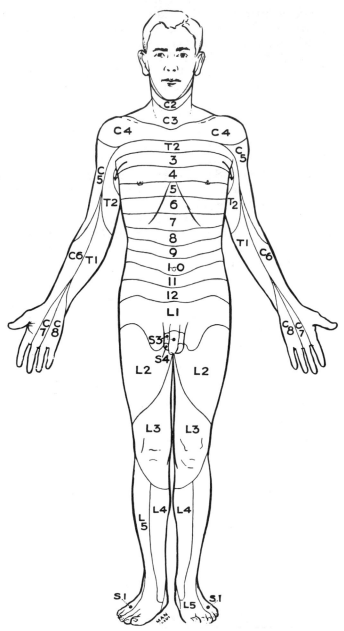

FIG. 2A. Dermatome map. Segmental innervation of the skin from anterior aspect. The uppermost dermatome adjoins the cutaneous field of the mandibular division of the trigeminal nerve. Arrows indicate lateral extensions of dermatome T3. (Adapted from Haymaker and Woodhall: Peripheral Nerve Injuries, 1953. Courtesy of W. B. Saunders.)

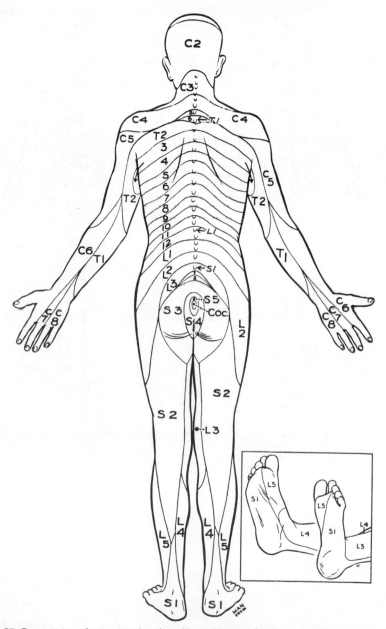

FIG. 2B. Dermatomes from posterior view. Note absence of cutaneous innervation by the first cervical segment. Arrows in the axillary regions indicate the lateral extent of dermatome T3. Those in the region of the vertebral column point to the thoracic, first lumbar, and first sacral spinous processes. (Adapted from Haymaker and Woodhall: Peripheral Nerve Injuries, 1953. Courtesy of W. B. Saunders.)

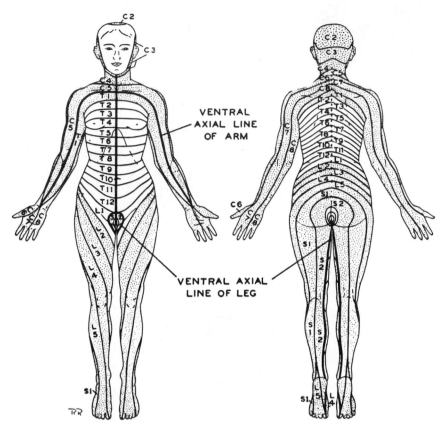

FIG. 3. Dermatome map. (From Keesan and Garrett: Anat Rec 102:411, 1948.)

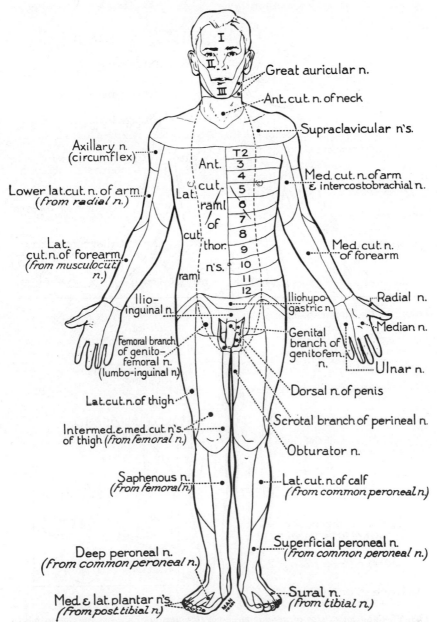

FIG. 4A. *Cutaneous fields of peripheral nerves from anterior aspect.* Numbers on the left side of the trunk refer to the intercostal nerves. On the right side are shown the cutaneous fields of the lateral and medial branches of the anterior primary rami. The asterisk just beneath the scrotum is in the field of the posterior cutaneous nerve of the thigh. (Adapted from Haymaker and Woodhall: Peripheral Nerve Injuries, 1953. Courtesy of W. B. Saunders.)

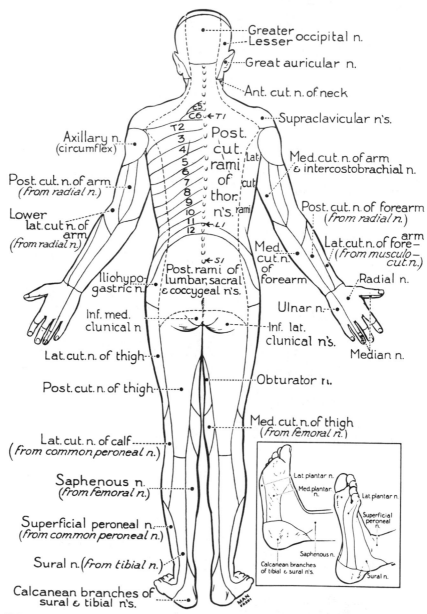

FIG. 4B. *Cutaneous fields of peripheral nerves from posterior aspect.* The boundaries of cutaneous supply of the posterior primary rami are indicated by broken lines. The designation *Post. cut. rami of thor. n's.* refers to the cutaneous branches of the posterior primary rami; *Lat. cut. rami* indicates the distribution from the lateral branches of the anterior primary rami. For purposes of orientation, the spinous processes of the first thoracic (T1), first lumbar (L1), and first sacral (S1) vertebrae are indicated by arrows. (Adapted from Haymaker and Woodhall: Peripheral Nerve Injuries, 1953. Courtesy of W. B. Saunders.)

TABLE 1

Diseases That Produce Pain Insensitivity and Hereditary Sensory Neuropathies

TYPE	HEREDITARY SENSORY RADICULAR NEUROPATHY (HSNI)	HEREDITARY SENSORY NEUROPATHY (HSNII)	FAMILIAL DYSAUTONOMIA (HSNIII)	HEREDITARY (FAMILIAL) SENSORY NEUROPATHY WITH ANHYDROSIS (HSNIV)	CONGENITAL INDIFFERENCE
Inheritance	Dominant	Recessive	Recessive (Jew)	Recessive	
Age at onset	2nd to 3rd decade	Infancy	Infancy	Infancy	Infancy
Deafness	May be present	May be present	Normal	Normal	Normal
Postural hypotension	Absent	Absent	Present	?	Normal
Incontinence	Absent	Absent	Present	?	Normal
Sense of touch	Early present, late absent	Absent	Present	Present	Normal
Deep tendon reflexes	Decreased at ankle	All reflexes	Absent	Normal	Normal
Sweating and flushing	Normal	Decreased sweating	Excessive sweating and flushing	Anhydrosis	Normal
Temperature control	Normal	Normal	Abnormal	Abnormal	Normal
Intelligence	Normal, but may be demented	Normal	May be subnormal	Retarded	Normal
Pathology	No myelinated nerve fibers; increase of Schwann cells; amyloid in spinal ganglia	No myelinated nerve fibers	Abnormalities of brainstem reticular formation; demyelination of dorsal roots	Absent Lissauer's tract and few small fibers	?

4
Abnormalities of Tone, Posture, Coordination, and Movement

ABNORMALITIES OF TONE

Hypotonia

Hypotonia is decreased resistance to passive movement, usually from disease of the anterior horn cells, motor nerve, muscle, or proprioceptive pathways. It is usually associated with joint hypermobility and decreased reflexes. See Chapter 12 for hypotonia of infancy.

Anterior horn cell
  Poliomyelitis
  Progressive spinal-muscular atrophy
  Syringomyelia
Peripheral nerve
  See neuropathies (Chap. 2)
Muscle
  See myopathies, neuromuscular junction, periodic paralysis, metabolic disturbances (Chap. 2)

Proprioceptive loss
  Anesthesia
  Tabes dorsalis
  Pernicious anemia
  Cerebellar disease (see Table 13)

Hypertonia

Hypertonia is increased resistance to passive movement, not caused by joint immobility or musculotendinous contractures, resulting from disease above the anterior horn cell.

Rigidity (lead pipe or waxy rigidity): increased tone in opposing muscle groups that causes a fairly steady resistance to passive motion throughout the range of movement, independent of the speed of manipulation, indicating extrapyramidal system dysfunction.

1. Cogwheel rigidity: extrapyramidal rigidity with intermittent lapses of muscle tension giving the sensation of a ratchet. This is often associated with Parkinson disease.

2. Gegenhalten (paratonic rigidity): stiffening of the limb against the direction of passive movement, seemingly as the result of contact. The reverse phenomenon where the patient is always moving his limb in the direction of passive manipulation is probably more frequent. They are likely related and seem to be more common in frontal lobe disturbances that interrupt connections to the basal ganglia. Gegenhalten is frequently associated with frontal lobe behavioral disorders (see Chap. 6).

3. Decerebrate rigidity: sustained contraction of all extensors (antigravity muscles). This was classically produced by an intercollicular lesion in cats (Sherringtonian rigidity), but it occurs with any extensive lesion from superior colliculus to vestibular nuclei.

4. Decorticate rigidity: contraction of extensors in the lower extremities and flexors in the upper extremities from any destructive lesion above collicular level.

Spasticity: increased tension in a muscle dependent on the speed of passive stretch. Classically this was thought to result from pyramidal involvement, but it is now thought to be dependent on pyramidal and extrapyramidal dysfunction causing imbalance of alpha-gamma control, resulting in an exaggeration of the muscle stretch reflex. This is distinguished from rigidity by its variation with speed of stretch, by a sudden release after the shortening response (clasp-knife response) caused by Golgi tendon organ discharge inhibiting the agonist, and by usually being more striking in upper extremity flexors and lower extremity extensors. This is usually secondary to destructive lesions above the collicular level. Diseases which cause spasticity are often associated with UMN weakness (see Chap. 2).

Dystonia

Dystonia is an abnormal limb position from sustained contraction of electromyographically normal motor units. This is an alpha-type rigidity, since dorsal root section does not interfere with its presence. See Table 1 for etiologies of various dystonic postures.

Muscle Spasms and Cramps

A muscle cramp is an involuntary painful muscle contraction that is transient. The contraction is accompanied by EMG evidence of muscle activity, thus distinguishing it from contractures. The sites of some cramp states can be found in Table 2. The etiology of muscle cramps is found in Table 3. The treatment of muscle cramps is found in Table 4. There are several persistent muscle contraction syndromes. The differential diagnosis among these syndromes is listed in Table 5. Occasionally some of the myopathies may be confused with the persistent muscle contraction states tetany and rigidity. The differential diagnosis of these is in Table 6.

ABNORMAL MOVEMENTS

Extrapyramidal disorders not only produce abnormal tone but also disturb movement. There may be a paucity of movement and decreased associated movements. The most striking feature may be an abnormal involuntary movement. This may be athetosis, ballismus, chorea, or various tremors. Athetosis results from simultaneous firing of agonists and antagonists, thus producing writhing, virtually continuous movements of the hands, lips, jaw, tongue, feet, or neck, in order of decreasing frequency. The differential diagnosis of diseases that cause athetosis can be found in Table 7. Chorea also has a similar predilection for distal involvement, but it results from sequential firing of agonists and antagonists, producing quick jerky movements. The differential diagnosis of chorea is given in Table 8. Ballismus is a violent flinging of limbs, with a pathologic substrate of subthalamic involvement. The differential diagnosis is given in Table 9. Tremors are rhythmic repetitions of movements at regular intervals. These may be physiologic, static (resting), postural (sustention), or intention in type. See Table 10 for a differential diagnosis of tremor. The etiologies of classic tremors are presented in Table 11. The treatment of abnormal movement is found in Table 12.

ATAXIA AND INCOORDINATION

The symptoms ataxia and incoordination can be seen from both central and peripheral sensory defects (also see gait disorders). In the absence of sensory disorders, cerebellar disease is the most common cause of dysfunction. Cerebellar disease may present in several different ways:

Cerebellar signs
  Hemispheric disease
    Hypotonia (not only is there decrease in tone, but there may be spooning of extended upper extremity)
    Adiadochokinesia (inability to perform rapidly alternating movements)
    Rebound
    Decompensation of movement
    Hypermetria
    Head tilt (head is tilted toward side of lesion, chin away from lesion)
    Side-to-side tremor (see Table 10 for differential diagnosis of tremor)
  Vermis
    Ataxia of trunk
    Broad-based gait
  Other
    Nystagmus (increase with fixations and on looking to side of lesion)
    Scanning speech
    Skew deviation
  Noncerebellar signs (produced by cerebellar disease)
    Signs of increased CSF pressure and hydrocephalus (see Chapter 8)
    Neck stiffness, posterior headache, suboccipital tenderness

Cerebellar signs and symptoms may be produced by a variety of etiologies. These are listed in Table 13. In addition to those diseases listed in Table 13, there are many familial and hereditary diseases which may produce cerebellar signs and symptoms. These are listed in Table 14.

MYOCLONUS

Myoclonus is an involuntary rapid contraction of a muscle or group of muscles that is repetitive but irregular. Myoclonus may be segmental or generalized. The etiologies of segmental myoclonus can be found in Table 15. The differential diagnosis of generalized myoclonus is given in Table 16. Table 17 contains the laboratory studies that may help to determine the etiology underlying the mycclonus.

ABNORMALITIES OF GAIT

Occasionally a patient may complain of difficulty walking, and an essential portion of any neurologic examination is observation of a patient's gait. Gait should be observed while the patient is walking spontaneously, and, if possible, the patient should be asked to perform tandem gait and to walk on his heels and toes. Frequently an observation of gait will help to determine the locus and nature of a patient's disability. Occasionally, additional neurologic tests are needed to help separate several similar types of gait disorders. Table 18 is a list of the most common neurologic gait disorders. Included in this list are (1) a description of the gait, (2) a description of various neurologic signs that may accompany each gait and help differentiate it from other gaits, and (3) a list of diseases associated with each gait.

TABLE 1
Differential Diagnosis of Dystonia

FLEXION DYSTONIA Sustained four-limb flexion posture referred to as the pallidal syndrome

Degenerative
Idiopathic Parkinson's disease (prototype)
Wilson's disease (terminal)
Huntington's chorea (terminal)
Alzheimer's disease (late)
Pick's disease
Olivopontocerebellar atrophy
Hunt's pallidal degeneration
Hallervorden-Spatz syndrome
Amyotrophic lateral sclerosis

Toxic
Carbon monoxide
Carbon disulfide
Phenothiazines
Cyanide
Nitrous oxide anesthesia
Manganese
Lead
Kernicterus

Metabolic
Pseudohypoparathyroidism
Pseudopseudohypoparathyroidism
Fahr's disease (idiopathic calcification of basal ganglia)
Hypoparathyroidism
Anoxia

Vascular
Diffuse vessel disease

Infectious
Meningitis, any etiology
Lues
Tuberculosis
Postencephalitic Parkinson's disease
Encephalitis, any etiology
Jakob-Creutzfeldt disease

Traumatic
Extensive damage to cortex or connections to globus pallidus

HEMIPLEGIC DYSTONIA Flexed upper and extended lower extremities without spasticity and often associated with athetosis; referred to as the striatal syndrome caudate—putamen or corticostriatal involvement

Degenerative
Juvenile Wilson's disease
Some Parkinson's disease
Huntington's chorea
Shy-Drager syndrome
Mild dystonia musculorum deformans
Striatonigral degeneration
Olivopontocerebellar atrophy

TABLE 1 (CONT.)

Differential Diagnosis of Dystonia

Toxic
  Manganese
  Methanol
  Phenothiazines

Metabolic
  Anoxia
  Subacute necrotizing encephalomyelitis (Leigh's disease)
  Hepatic encephalopathy

Vascular
  Venous stasis in vein of Galen or thalamostriate distribution associated
      with birth trauma (anoxia)

Infectious
  Jakob-Creutzfeldt disease
  Postencephalitic Parkinson's disease

Traumatic
  Severe head trauma of later life
  Birth trauma with anoxia leading to status marmoratus

SPASTIC DYSTONIA The same posture as in hemiplegic dystonia, but
with associated spasticity, ie, combined extrapyramidal and pyramidal
disease

Degenerative
  Familial spastic paraplegia

Metabolic
  Anoxia
  Hypoglycemia

Vascular
  Thrombosis
  Embolus
  Intracerebral hemorrhage (most common site is putamen)
  Vasculitis

TORSION DYSTONIA: Attitude of decerebrate rigidity
  Tentorial herniation
  Dystonia musculorum deformans

TABLE 2

Sites of Some Muscle Cramp States

CAUSE OF CRAMPS	TREAT-MENT
Central	
Questionable increased norepinephrine suprasegmental influence, eg, stiff-man syndrome	Valium
Cord	
Central interneuron damage Neurotransmitter–Gaba	
Gaba inhibited by picrotoxin, biculline, tetanus toxin	Valium
(Tetanus and stiff-man syndrome may be from central interneuron damage)	
Renshaw cell damage	
Neurotransmitter to anterior horn cell–glycine for inhibition	
Glycine inhibited by strychnine, tetanus toxin	
Renshaw cells destroyed by poliomyelitis	
(Tetanus and stiff-man syndrome may be from Renshaw cell damage)	
Diseases of Anterior Horn Cell	
Amyotrophic lateral sclerosis (ALS)	
Partial Denervation	
Specific Distal Axon Excitability	
Isaacs-Mertens syndrome, blackwidow spider bite (acetylcholine release), probably fasciculations	Dilantin and Tegretol
Excitable Muscle Side of Neuromuscular Junction	
Schwartz-Jampel syndrome	Dilantin
Excitable Muscle Membrane	
Myotonia	Quinine, procaineamide
Muscle	
Glycogenoses	
Carnitine	
Calcium disturbance	
Decreased relaxing factor	

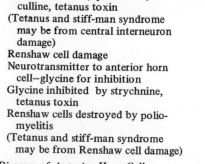
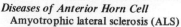
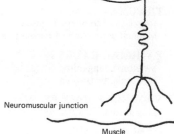

Internuncial

Presynaptic inhibition

Postsynaptic inhibition

Glycine

Anterior horn cell

ACH

Renshaw cell

Neuromuscular junction

Muscle

TABLE 3

Etiology of Muscle Cramps

INFECTIONS
Clostridium tetani
Poliomyelitis (remote)

TOXIC–METABOLIC CAUSES
Uremia
Energy (ATP) depletion preventing relaxation
  Rigor mortis
Glycogen storage disorders
  McArdle's disease (phosphorylase deficiency)
  Phosphofructokinase deficiency
  Phosphohexoisomerase deficiency
  Carnitine deficiency (carnitine palmityl transferase deficiency)
Tetany
  Hypocalcemia
  Alkalosis
  Hypomagnesemia
Diazacholesterol (myotonia)
Clofibrate (cramps)
Hyponatremia
Dichlorophenoxyacetic acid (2,4-D) (persistent muscle contraction)
Hypothyroidism (Debré-Semelaigne)
Addison's disease
Pregnancy
Hyperkalemic periodic paralysis with myotonia (paramyotonia congenita)
Strychnine
Black-widow spider bite

TRAUMA
Direct blow to normal muscle
Minimal percussion of partially denervated (regenerating nerve) muscle

FAMILIAL CAUSES
Myotonia congenita
Myotonia dystrophia

VASCULAR CAUSES
Intermittent claudication

OTHER CAUSES
Nocturnal cramps, especially of elderly
Writer's cramp
Dystonias (see previous section)
Severe exercise
Pregnancy
Partial denervation of any cause (ALS is prominent early symptom; may occur in other
  peripheral neuropathies)
Myopathies, including polymyositis
Myokymias
Stiff-man syndrome
Benign fasciculations
Adolescent familial cramps

TABLE 4

Treatment of Muscle Cramps

ORIGIN	TREATMENT
Central	Valium, 5 mg t.i.d. to q.i.d., upper limit determined by side effects
Peripheral nerve	Dilantin, 300–400 mg q.d. Tegretol, 200 mg b.i.d. to 300 mg q.i.d.
Muscle component of neuromuscular junction	Dilantin, 300–400 mg q.d.
Muscle membrane (eg, myotonia, many metabolic cramps, nocturnal cramps of elderly)	Quinine, 300–600 mg b.i.d. to t.i.d. Procaineamide, up to 1 g q.i.d. Dilantin, 300–400 mg q.d.
Uncouple excitation and contraction at sarcoplasmic reticulum (for relief of spasticity at expense of strength; not applicable for muscle spasm)	Dantrium, 25 mg b.i.d. to 100 mg q.i.d.

TABLE 5

Persistent Muscle Contraction Syndromes

SYMPTOM OR SIGN	STIFF-MAN SYNDROME	ISAACS-MERTENS SYNDROME	SCHWARTZ-JAMPEL SYNDROME	MYOTONIA
Muscle activity during sleep or anesthesia	0	+	+	+ to percussion
Muscle activity after peripheral nerve block	0	+ but decreasing as block is placed more distal	+	+ to percussion
Muscle activity after curare	0	0	0	+ to percussion
EMG insertional activity	Normal	Normal	Increased	Increased
Site	Central: suprasegmental (questionable increased norepinephrine influence); questionable Gaba system; questionable Renshaw cells; internuncial cord, glycine system	Peripheral nerve with greatest effect distally, perhaps from abnormally increased acetylcholine release	Muscle portion of neuro-muscular junction	Muscle membrane

TABLE 6

Differentiating Features of Increased Tone in Myopathies, Tetany, Rigidity, and Persistent Muscle Contraction States

CONDITION	INHERITANCE	USUAL ONSET	EMG DURING CRAMPS	PAIN	EFFECT OF EXERCISE ON CRAMPS	EFFECT OF ISCHEMIA ON CRAMPS	EXERCISE LACTATE	EFFECT OF COLD ON CRAMPS
Tetany	None	Any age	Sustained activity; doublets, triplets	In advanced stages	↑	↑	Should be normal	?
Glycogenoses								
McArdle's	Probably autosomal recessive	Childhood	Silent	+	↑	↑	No ↑	?
Phosphofructokinase	Probably autosomal recessive	Childhood	Silent	+	↑	↑	No ↑	?
Phosphohexoisomerase	Probably autosomal recessive	Childhood	Silent	+	↑	No effect	No ↑	?
Decreased relaxing factor	?	Childhood	Silent	0	↑	0	↑ at rest and normal ↑ with exercise	↑

TABLE 6 (CONT.)

Differentiating Features of Increased Tone in Myopathies, Tetany, Rigidity, and Persistent Muscle Contraction States

CONDITION	INHERITANCE	USUAL ONSET	EMG DURING CRAMPS	PAIN ON CRAMPS	EXERCISE ON CRAMPS	EFFECT OF ISCHEMIA ON CRAMPS	EXERCISE LACTATE	EFFECT OF COLD ON CRAMPS
Carnitine deficiency	Autosomal recessive	Childhood	?	+	↑	?	Normal ↑	?
Myotonias								
Congenita (Thomsen)	Autosomal dominant	Childhood (early)	Waxing/waning	0	↓	0	Normal ↑	↑
Congenita (Becker)	Autosomal recessive	Childhood (early)						
Dystrophia	Autosomal dominant	Adult						
Hyperkalemia	Autosomal dominant	Childhood						
Persistent muscle contraction (myokymia)		Continuous activity			↑	?	Normal	?
Isaacs-Mertens syndrome	Sporadic	Any age		0				
Schwartz-Jampel syndrome	Autosomal recessive	Childhood		0				
Stiff-man syndrome	Sporadic	Any age		+				
Spasticity or rigidity		Silent						

TABLE 7

Differential Diagnosis of Diseases That Cause Athetosis

DEGENERATIVE/FAMILIAL DISEASES
Hallervorden-Spatz disease
Progressive pallidal atrophy
Tuberous sclerosis
Paroxysmal choreoathetosis (not progressive)
Wilson's disease (transient)
Pelizaeus-Merzbacher disease (demyelinating)
Pick's disease

TOXIC CAUSES
Hyperbilirubinemias
  Kernicterus
  Bile duct atresia
  Sepsis
  Excess vitamin K
  Sulfonamides
  Glucuronide conjugation defects
  Hepatitis
  Congenital lues
  Cytomegalic inclusion disease
Carbon monoxide
Carbon disulfide
Manganese
Lithium
Barbiturates

METABOLIC DISEASES
Birth anoxia
Lesch-Nyhan syndrome
Tay-Sachs disease
Phenylketonuria
Louis-Bar syndrome

VASCULAR DISEASES
Usually hemiathetosis
Residual of infantile hemiplegia
Emboli

INFECTIONS
Measles
Pertussis
Diphtheria
Smallpox
Lues
Tuberculoma
Encephalitis

TRAUMA
Birth trauma with asphyxia/anoxia

NEOPLASM
Rare cause of hemiathetosis

PSEUDOATHETOSIS
Result of severe proprioceptive sensory loss

TABLE 8

Differential Diagnosis of Chorea

DEGENERATIVE DISEASES
Huntington's chorea
Wilson's disease
Louis-Bar syndrome (ataxia-telangiectasia)
Pick's disease
Sturge-Weber syndrome
Senility

TOXIC CAUSES
Alcoholism
Phenothiazines (Stelazine > Thorazine > Mellaril)
Butyrophenone (Haldol)
L-dopa
INH
Reserpine
Amphetamines
Oral contraceptives
Carbon monoxide
Hyoscyamine
Hyperbilirubinemias
Lithium
Mercury
Burn encephalopathy of children

METABOLIC DISEASES
Cerebral lipidoses
Phenylketonuria
Vitamin B_{12} deficiency of infants
Porphyria
Hypomagnesemia
Addison's disease
Hypoparathyroidism
Other hypocalcemias
Hypoglycemia
Thyrotoxicosis

VASCULAR DISEASES
Sydenham's chorea
Thrombotic/embolic disease
Arteritis
Chorea gravidarum
Polycythemia

INFECTIONS
Sydenham's chorea
Varicella
Typhoid
Pertussis
Measles
Diphtheria
Mumps
Lues

TRAUMA

NEOPLASTIC DISEASES
Thalamic gliomas
Microgliomatosis

TABLE 9

Differential Diagnosis of Ballismus

DEGENERATIVE DISEASE
　Demyelinating disease

VASCULAR DISEASES
　Thrombosis
　Embolus
　Vasculitis

INFECTIONS
　Syphillis
　Tuberculoma
　Abscess
　Encephalitis

TRAUMA

NEOPLASM
　Metastatic

TABLE 10

Differential Diagnosis of Tremor

TYPE OF TREMOR	PRESENT WITH INTENTION	PRESENT RESTING	PRESENT WITH SUSTENTION	TYPE OF TREMOR	TONE CHANGES	ASSOCIATED SIGNS
Cerebellar	+	0	0	At right angles to movement; increases as subject approaches target	Hypotonia	See text on previous pages
Essential (benign, familial, senile)	+	0	+	Appears to be in direction of movement (tappinglike)	0	Titubation
Parkinson's	0	+	0̂	Pill-rolling type	Plastic or cogwheel rigidity	Hypokinesia
Rubral	+	+	+	On intention, looks cerebellar; on resting, rotary or flexion-extension	Hypotonia	May have mesencephalic signs
Metabolic	+	±	+	Rapid and fine	0	Rapid pulse, fever, etc

TABLE 11

Etiology of Tremor

PHYSIOLOGIC TREMOR

Physiologic tremor is a tremor that is normally present with varying amplitude and a frequency that varies, with age, between 5 and 15 cycles per second. It is present in sustention and movement, but not at rest.

ABNORMAL TREMORS

Static
  Parkinson's disease
  Parkinson syndromes have been produced by:
    Toxins
      Reserpine
      Aldomet
      Phenothiazines
      Cyanide
      Butyrophenone
      Manganese
      Carbon monoxide
    Infections
      von Economo's encephalitis
      In acute phase of infection with:
        Measles
        Chickenpox
        Japanese B encephalitis
        Western equine encephalitis
        Coxsackie B
  Parkinson syndromes have been thought to be secondary to other causes, but this has not been proved:
    Arteriosclerosis
    Electric shock
    Trauma
    Emotional trauma
  Some other system degenerations may have Parkinsonian features:
    Supranuclear palsy of Steele-Richardson-Olzewski
    Orthostatic hypotension of Shy-Drager
    Olivopontocerebellar atrophy
  Rubral tremor is reportedly a resting tremor that does not disappear, or even worsens with intention

Postural
  Physiologic variants (adrenalin injection will give this tremor of greater amplitude)
    Anxiety
    Fatigue
    Withdrawal
    Thyrotoxicosis
    Benign essential tremor
  Nonphysiologic
    Cerebellar postural lapses, titubation, overswing asterixis (EMG silence during postural lapse followed by firing as hand is returned to fixed posture)
      Hepatic failure
      Uremia
      Steatorrhea
      Hypokalemia
      Hypomagnesemia
      CO_2 narcosis
      Polycythemia with heart failure

Intention
  Cerebellum (see Table 13)

TABLE 12

Treatment of Abnormal Movements

PARKINSON'S DISEASE

Dopaminergic
Sinemet: Start with ½ of a 25/250 tablet t.i.d. and increase by ½ tablet q.o.d. to a maximum of 8 tablets q.d.
L-dopa: 250 mg t.i.d. with meals, with an increase of 250 mg every 4 days to a maximum dose of 8 g q.d.
Symmetrel: 100 mg q.d. for 2 weeks followed by 100 mg b.i.d.; increases of 100 mg can be made every 2 weeks to maximum dose of 400 mg.

Antihistaminic
Benadryl: 50–150 mg q.d.

Anticholinergics
Akineton: 1–2 mg t.i.d. (increase slowly)
Artane: 1 mg q.d., followed by increasing dosage by 2 mg every 5 days to a total of 15 mg in three divided doses.
Cogentin: 0.5 mg h.s., with an increase of 0.5 mg every third night to a maximum dose of 6 mg.

ANXIETY: psychotherapy and medications (eg, Valium 5 mg q.i.d.)

FATIGUE, WITHDRAWAL, THYROTOXICOSIS: treat underlying etiology

BENIGN ESSENTIAL TREMOR
Propranolol: 10 mg t.i.d., with an increase of 10 mg q.d. every 4 days to a maximum of 160 mg (40 mg q.i.d.)

TABLE 13

Differential Diagnosis of Some Diseases That Produce Cerebellar Signs and Symptoms

ETIOLOGY	SYMPTOMS
Extra-axial Tumors	
Neuromas	Frequently, first sign is cranial nerve abnormalities (ie,
Meningiomas	VIII, V); also may present with ipsilateral cerebellar signs; tumors near the foramen magnum may present with bilateral pyramidal and cerebellar signs with nystagmus (downbeat)
Intra-axial Tumors	
Metastatic	The cerebellum is a common area for metastatic tumors (ie, lung, breast, melanoma, kidney); metastatic tumors most frequently present with cerebellar hemispheric signs, but may also present with vermal or noncerebellar signs
Astrocytoma	Most common glioma of children; rare in adults; may present with hemispheric or vermal signs; prognosis excellent with surgery
Medulloblastoma	Occurs mainly in early childhood (3–6 years); frequently presents with noncerebellar signs; may involve cranial nerves or spinal roots
Hemangioblastoma	May be associated with Von Reckinghausen's disease, Von Hippel-Lindau's disease, polycythemia; occurs mainly in adults, and usually presents with hemispheric or vermal signs
Remote effect	Seen most frequently with carcinoma of lung
Vascular Disease	
Atherosclerosis	Sudden onset, usually associated with brainstem signs, may require neurosurgical decompression (see Chapter 9)
Hemorrhage	Sudden onset, nausea and vomiting, nystagmus, ataxia, loss of consciousness, small pupils, hyperventilation; accounts for about 10% of intracerebral bleeds; requires immediate neurosurgical decompression (see Chapter 11, Table 4)
Vasculitis	Similar to atherosclerosis; may be associated with systemic lupus erythematosus, polyarteritis nodosa, temporal arteritis, and other forms of vasculitis
Developmental and Structural Defects	
Arnold-Chiari malformation	May be associated with syrinx and hydrocephalus; may first produce symptoms during adulthood
Basilar impression	Produces decreased size of posterior fossa; can be diagnosed with plain x-rays
Demyelination	
Multiple sclerosis	Usually produces hemispheric signs; however, may produce vermal signs
Degenerative and familial diseases	See Table 14

TABLE 13 (CONT.)

ETIOLOGY	SYMPTOMS
Toxins, deficiencies, physical states	
Dilantin	Usually dose-related, but may be irreversible; usually presents with nystagmus, vermal signs, dysarthria
Alcohol	Probably caused in part by thiamine deficiency; mainly vermal; may be associated with other signs of Wernicke-Korsakoff's syndrome
Mercury	Frequently associated with neuropathy, dementia, amyotrophy
Vitamin B_{12}	Usually myelopathy and neuropathy more prominent, but there may be cerebellar signs
Heat stroke and high fever	May appear several days after episode; usually bilateral ataxia and dysmetria and incoordination
Hypoxia and/or hypoglycemia	Usually bilaterally symmetric
Infections	
Viral	Cerebellum may be involved with almost any virus; in children, may also occur acutely after virus (ie, coxsackie, echo, measles, chickenpox); this acute ataxia is usually a self-limited disease
Bacterial abscess	Next to temporal lobe, most common area of abscess; may show hemispheric or vermal signs, and may present like a mass lesion
Other	Cerebellum may be involved by syphilis, trichinosis, typhus, and many other infections
Endocrine disorder	
Hypothyroidism	Hypothyroid patient may be ataxic; appears to have vermal dysfunction; associated with systemic signs of hypothyroidism
Childhood ataxia	
Louis-Barr syndrome (ataxia-telangiectasia)	Hereditary ataxia, begins in childhood; associated with telangiectasia of eyes and skin
Hartnup's disease	Cerebellar ataxia associated with skin eruptions, mental retardation, and aminoaciduria
Bassen-Kornzweig syndrome (abetalipoproteinemia)	Spinocerebellar degeneration with retardation, aleatorrhea, retinitis pigmentosa; blood smears show acanthocytes
Other (gangliosidosis, leukodystrophies, and aminoaciduria) (see Chapter 8)	

TABLE 14

Familial and Hereditary Diseases with Cerebellar Signs

DISEASE	INHERITANCE AND ONSET	COURSE	PYRAMIDAL SIGNS	PERIPHERAL NERVE	NYSTAGMUS	DEMENTIA	CRANIAL NERVE ABNORMALITY	POSTERIOR COLUMN	OTHER
Spinocerebellar									
Friedreich's ataxia	Autosomal recessive 7–8 years	Moderate, 10–20 years	++	+++	+++	±	Occasional optic atrophy	++++	Pes cavus; scoliosis; cardiac abnormalities
Marie-Sanger-Brown ataxia	Autosomal dominant Adult	Slow	+++	±	+	±	Optic atrophy	±	
Roussy-Lévy disease	Autosomal dominant Adult	Slow	0	+++ (muscle atrophy)	0	0	Optic atrophy	++	Pes cavus; scoliosis
Refsum's disease	Autosomal recessive Early adult	Rapid to slow	0	+++	+	0	Blinding retinitis pigmentosa; decreased hearing	+	Cardiac changes; ichthyosis; phytanic acid

TABLE 14 (CONT.)

Familial and Hereditary Diseases with Cerebellar Signs

DISEASE	INHERITANCE AND ONSET	COURSE	PYRAMIDAL SIGNS	PERIPHERAL NERVE	NYSTAGMUS	DEMENTIA	CRANIAL NERVE ABNORMALITY	POSTERIOR COLUMN	OTHER
Olivopontocerebellar									
Dejerine-Thomas	Sporadic Adult	Rapid, <10 years	+	0	++	++	0	+	
Menzel	Dominant Adult	Moderate, 10–20 years	+	+	++	++	Optic atrophy and eye movements abnormal	+	May have pes cavus and scoliosis
Cerebellar Ataxia									
Holmes	Dominant Adult	Moderate	0	0	++	0	0	0	May have hypogonadism
Ramsay-Hunt	Sporadic Young adult	Slow	0	0	0	0	0	0	Myoclonic jerks

TABLE 15

Etiologies of Segmental Myoclonus

TYPE OF MYOCLONUS	SIGNS AND SYMPTOMS	UNDERLYING CAUSES
Singultus	Hiccups	Cerebrovascular disease Local irritation: diaphragmatic hernia; GI disturbances; aortic aneurysm; peritonitis; mediastinitis; pericarditis; pleurisy Toxins: uremia; sulfonamides Tumors: fourth ventricle; increased intracranial pressure; cord tumor Encephalitis
Opsoclonus	Conjugate, unequal continuous rapid eye movements	Idiopathic in children Remote effect of tumors (ie, neuroblastoma) Encephalitis Disorder of cerebellum Pelizaeus-Merzbacher disease
Palatal myoclonus	Rhythmic movement of oral-brachial respiratory muscles; may have ocular movement	Cerebrovascular disease (brainstem) Multiple sclerosis Brainstem tumors, atrioventricular malformation Syringobulbia Brainstem encephalitis
Jaw and face	Myokymia; hemifacial spasm	Idiopathic Multiple sclerosis (pontine) Brainstem tumor (pontine) Cerebrovascular disease
Spinal cord	Very rapid (20–200/minute) at or below level of cord involvement	Any lesion of cord (ie, tumor, trauma, demyelinating disease) (see Chapter 2)

TABLE 16

Differential Diagnosis of Generalized Myoclonus

ETIOLOGY	CLINICAL	LABORATORY AND PATHOLOGY	TREATMENT
Infections			
Viral	In von Economo's disease myoclonus may be periodic; myoclonus may be seen with a viral encephalitis; myoclonus may coexist with coma	LP; viral titers	
Dawson's inclusion encephalitis (SSPE)	Occurs in children (4–20 years); fatal in 3 months to 1 year; associated with mental deterioration and torsion movements	Type A intranuclear inclusions; EEG, burst suppression; measles titers	? amantadine
Jakob-Creutzfeldt disease	Seen in adults (4th–6th decades); rapid dementia with blindness, rigidity, ataxia, and myoclonus; may occur in families	Spongioform encephalopathy; can be transmitted in animals; EEG periodic slow and sharp wave activity	
Metabolic and Toxic Causes			
Uremia	Usually associated with decreased level of consciousness; may be multifocal	BUN	
Other	May be seen in all other causes of metabolic encephalopathy (see metabolic etiologies of coma, (Chapter 5, Table 5)	See Chapter 5, Table 1	
Toxic	Seen with strychnine poisoning, tetanus, heavy metals, and many other poisons		
Vascular and Hypoxic *(Action Myoclonus)*	Seen after hypoxic encephalopathy; more intense with intention		Serotonin precursors (5-HTP)? ? clonazedam ? L-dopa

Hereditary and Familial Diseases

Disease	Clinical features	Diagnosis/Treatment
Progressive myoclonus epilepsy (Unverricht) Lafora body type	Age of onset 10–20 years; rapidly progressive dementia, ataxia, generalized seizures	Biopsy liver, muscle, or brain
Lipidosis and leukodystrophies	Age of onset 10–20 years; rapidly progressive dementia, with ataxia, generalized seizures; rapidly fatal	Leukocytes, enzymes
Familial system degeneration (Ramsay-Hunt syndrome)	Age of onset before 10 years; may or may not be demented; may have ocular findings, seizures, and ataxia; may be rapidly fatal (see Chapter 13 for differential diagnosis	
	Onset after age 10 years; no progressive dementia but may be retarded; may have ataxia; no generalized seizures	
Wilson's disease	Frequently associated with extrapyramidal signs (see Chap. 4) and Kayser-Fleischer rings	Ceruloplasmin, urine amino acids, LFT's
Alzheimer's disease, senile dementia, and Pick's disease	May be associated with amnestic dementia, language and praxis disorders	Senile plaques, neurofibrillary tangles, lipofuscin deposits
Alper's disease	See Chapter 3	
Nonprogressive seizure disorders	15–70% of epileptics have occasional myoclonic jerks; EEG may be purely myoclonic, or can be associated with petit mal, grand mal, or psychomotor seizures	Treat underlying disease; anticonvulsants
Paramyoclonus Multiplex (Hereditary Essential Myoclonus or Friedreich's Essential Myoclonus)	Benign syndrome, autosomal dominant inheritance; no ataxia, no dementia, no seizures; normal EEG	

TABLE 17

Laboratory Studies in Myoclonus

BLOOD STUDIES

Glucose
Ca^{++} and electrolytes
BUN and creatinine
Blood gasses and PH
FTA
Liver function tests
Toxin screens*
Heavy metal screens*
T_4
Ceruloplasmin
Amino acids*

OTHER STUDIES

EEG
LP (protein, sugar, cells, viral titers, bacterial cultures, gamma globulin, VDRL)
Skull x-ray
Biopsy (ie, brain, liver, rectal, muscle, skin, depending on differential diagnosis)
CT scan
Myelogram with segmental myoclonus

Test urine also.

TABLE 18

Major Gait Disorders

HEMIPARETIC GAIT

Description: When a hemiparesis is very mild, a patient may have as his only sign a decrease in arm swing on the affected side. With a more severe hemiparesis, the arm is held in a flexed posture (flexion at shoulder, elbow, wrist), and the leg is held in an extension posture. The lower extremities also may be inverted, and when the patient walks, he circumducts his lower extremity.

Associated neurologic signs: Usually there is weakness on the affected side, hyperreflexia, and extensor plantar response.

Associated diseases: Hemiparetic gait is usually seen with hemispheric disease (Chapter 2, Table 3) but may be seen with brainstem disease (Chapter 2, Table 2) and with unilateral high cervical cord disease.

PARAPARETIC GAIT

Description: Paraparetic gait is commonly called the scissors gait because it looks as if the patient's legs are scissors. The lower extremities are stiff and tend to remain in an extension posture; at the same time, the lower extremities tend to remain adducted.

Associated neurologic signs: Bilateral weakness (especially flexors) of lower extremities, bilateral hyperreflexia and bilateral extensor plantar responses.

Associated diseases: See Chapter 2, Figure 1 and Tables 4 and 5. In addition, it may be seen with spastic diplegia of childhood (a form of cerebral palsy) and bilateral hemispheric disease (especially in parasagittal region) and brainstem disease.

SENSORY GAIT

Description: If the motor system is not involved, patients with a sensory gait (ie, tabes dorsalis) may appear normal when they are looking at their lower extremities, but become ataxic (wide base and poorly coordinated) when not looking at their lower extremities. These patients may even fall when visual input is withdrawn.

Associated neurologic signs: Patients have positive Romberg signs and decreased position sense.

Associated diseases: Sensory gait is most frequently associated with root disease and peripheral nerve disease.

STEPPAGE GAIT

Description: In order to overcome weakness of the foot dorsiflexors, these patients excessively flex at their hips and knees when walking; this may be unilateral or bilateral. When the subject cannot plantar flex the foot, the stride may also be decreased. In certain cases, stride may be decreased without a steppage gait if the plantar flexors are weak and the dorsiflexors are strong.

Associated neurologic signs: Weakness of foot dorsiflexors, atrophy of the anterior compartment of leg, sensory loss on lateral aspect of leg. With a decreased stride there may be atrophy and weakness of the calf muscles and decreased ankle jerk.

Associated diseases: Neuropathies, radiculopathies, and occasional myelopathies.

PETIT PAS GAIT, SLIPPING-CLUTCH GAIT, PULSIVE GAIT (BRUN'S APRAXIA)

Description: These three gaits will be discussed together because they may be seen in the same patient; however, frequently they may be isolated or in combination with one of the other gaits. The patient with a petit pas gait takes small steps. In the slipping-clutch gait the patient has difficulty initiating a step. It appears his feet are almost stuck to the floor. Once he moves out, however, he may demonstrate a petit pas gait or have a normal stride. In a pulsive (may also be retropulsive) gait, the patient's center of gravity appears to be either in front or behind him, and he is struggling to keep his feet up to his center of gravity.

TABLE 18 (CONT.)

Associated neurologic signs: Hypokinesia, increased tone (plastic or paratonic rigidity), grasp reflexes, suck and root reflexes, urinary incontinence, dementia, resting tremor.

Associated diseases: May be seen with diseases that produce frontal lobe signs; hydrocephalus; Parkinson's disease and related basal ganglial disorders. Frontal lobe ataxia (Brun's apraxia) may appear very similar to cerebellar ataxia. Both may demonstrate pulsion and retropulsion.

CEREBELLAR ATAXIA

Description: Patients with this gait walk with a wide base and appear to have poor coordination of movements (ataxia), decomposition of movements, and titubation. This gait is frequently confused with Brun's apraxia.

Associated neurologic signs: On the heel-to-knee test, patients will show ataxia (poor coordination). They will have dysmetria and will demonstrate intact position sense.

Associated diseases: Disease that affects the cerebellum (see Chapter 4, Table 13).

VERTIGINOUS GAIT

Description: The patients look like they are always falling to one side or look like they are walking on a ship at sea. This gait may be confused with gait of intoxication, hysteric gait, and cerebellar gait.

Associated neurologic signs: These patients will frequently have nystagmus.

Associated diseases: Usually associated with disorders of labyrinth, diseases of nerves, and brainstem disease (see Chapter 9).

INTOXICATED GAIT

Description: This looks very similar to the vertiginous gait. With certain intoxicants (ie, diphenylhydantoin) it may look more like cerebellar gait.

Associated neurologic signs: May also have nystagmus, but also has slow reaction time, decreased mental status, slurring of speech.

Associated diseases: Use of intoxicants.

HYSTERIC GAIT

Description: There are several varieties. Some hysteric patients will not bear weight despite adequate strength in their lower extremities. Others appear almost intoxicated and will stagger with fancy footwork and at the last moment catch on to something, but rarely fall and hurt themselves. Last, there are those who struggle making each step.

Associated neurologic signs: Hemisensory loss, Hoover's sign, tunnel vision, give-way weakness, and other signs of conversion.

Associated diseases: Psychogenic.

CHOREIFORM GAIT

Description: Chorea means dance, and this is the best description of this gait.

Associated neurologic signs: Athetotic and choreiform movements.

Associated diseases: Mainly basal ganglial diseases.

5
Coma

Coma is perhaps the most common medical emergency; it accounts for approximately 3 percent of admissions to large municipal hospitals. The comatose patient often is a major diagnostic and therapeutic challenge, because the history is not available and the neurologic examination is hampered by the patient's inability to cooperate. In spite of these difficulties, unless the physician makes the correct diagnosis and rapidly institutes therapy, the patient may either die or be left with permanent neurologic sequelae.

After it has been established that the patient has an adequate airway and is not in shock, diagnostic blood studies should be obtained (Table 1). In the absence of an obvious cause for the comatose state, such as head injury or meningitis, certain diagnoses require urgent treatment; otherwise, irreversible damage ensues. For example, such a patient should be given 50 ml of 50 percent dextrose intravenously and 200 mg of thiamine intramuscularly. Following this, the patient should undergo a general physical and neurologic examination. This examination should determine the patient's level of neurologic dysfunction, which can be used as a guide for the course of the illness (Table 2). The examination should also determine if the insult is more suggestive of a metabolic or structural process (Table 3). If it appears that the cause of coma is of metabolic origin, additional studies may be warranted, based on consideration of diagnostic possibilities (Table 4). If neurologic examination suggests a structural etiology, the different diagnoses to be considered include those in Table 5. Often the patient with structural disease will be diagnosed with the CT scan however special diagnostic studies such as arteriography or pneumoencephalography may be needed to make the diagnosis.

TABLE 1

Diagnostic Studies

INITIAL BLOOD STUDIES

Arterial PO_2, PCO_2, pH
Hematocrit, white blood cell count, differential count
Serum K^+, Na^+, Ca^{++}, Cl^-, CO_2, Mg^{++} glucose, T_4, BUN, barbiturates, bromides, blood alcohol, liver function studies
Blood culture

OTHER STUDIES

Neurodiagnostic

Skull x-rays
Echoencephalogram (unless pineal gland is calcified)
EEG
Brain scan or computer tomography
Lumbar puncture (unless contraindicated because of evidence of intracranial hypertension)

Other

Chest x-ray
EKG

TABLE 2

Level of Dysfunction

SIGNS AND SYMPTOMS	CEREBRAL	SUBCORTICAL	MIDBRAIN	PONS	MEDULLA
Consciousness	Normal or akinetic mutism (bilateral cingulate gyrus)	Lethargy and apathy (thalamus); drowsiness (hypothalamus)	Coma	Coma	
Respiration	Normal or posthyperventilation apnea	Cheyne-Stokes	Central hyperventilation	Apneustic or cluster	Atactic
Pupils	Normal	Small and reactive	Nuclear: midposition and fixed III nerve: unilateral dilated and fixed Pretectal: large fixed	Pinpoint	Horner's syndrome (lateral medulla)
Eye movements at rest	Roving eye movements, or look toward destructive lesion and away from paretic side	Roving eye movements, or look toward destructive lesion	III nerve: eye down and out	Look away from lesion and toward paretic side	
Doll's eyes and caloric stimulation	Present	Present	Absent or abnormal response	Absent or abnormal response	
Motor	Hemiparesis	Decortication	Decerebration	Decerebration (rostral pons)	

TABLE 3

Differential Diagnosis Between Metabolic and Structural Causes of Coma*

CRANIAL NERVES	METABOLIC	STRUCTURAL
II Nerve		
Blink to threat	Equal	Asymmetric
Disks	Flat, good pulsation	Papilledema
III, IV, VI Nerves		
Extraocular movement	Roving eye movements; normal doll's eyes and calorics	Gaze paresis, III nerve, MLF syndrome (internuclear ophthalmoplegia)
Pupils	Equal and reactive; may be large (ie, atropine), pin-point (ie, opiates), or mid-position and fixed (ie, Doriden)	Asymmetric and/or non-reactive
V Nerve		
Corneal reflex	Symmetric response	Asymmetric response
VII Nerve		
Grimace to pain	Symmetric response	Asymmetric response
Motor Function		
Movement	Symmetric	Asymmetric
Tone	Symmetric	Paratonic, spastic, flaccid, especially if asymmetric
Posture	Symmetric	Decorticate, especially if asymmetric; decerebrate, especially if asymmetric
Deep tendon reflexes	Symmetric	Asymmetric
Babinski sign	Absent or symmetric	Present
Sensation	Symmetric	Asymmetric

*This table is to serve as a general guide, because one can occasionally see patients with structural disease who initially appeared to have metabolic disease. This is especially true with chronic subdural hematomas. Therefore, all comatose patients who are suspected of having a metabolic etiology should at least undergo skull x-ray, echoencephalogram, EEG, and radioisotope scan or computer tomography. They should also be observed to make certain they do not deteriorate or develop focal signs.

TABLE 4

Coma from Causes Other than Mass Lesions

INFECTIONS

Meningitis
Encephalitis

METABOLIC CAUSES

Hypoxia (normal cerebral blood flow)
 Decreased atmospheric O_2
 Pulmonary disease
 Hypoventilation
 Anemia
 CO poisoning
 Methemoglobinemia

Ischemia (decreased cerebral blood flow)
 Decreased cardiac output
  Arrhythmias
  Atrial myxoma
  Valvular disease
  Acute myocardial infarction
 Generalized fall of blood pressure
  Hypovolemic
  Vasovagal
  Carotid sinus
  Pulmonary embolus
  Dissecting aneurysm
  Sepsis
  Orthostatic
 Increased vascular resistance
  Hypertensive encephalopathy
  Polycythemia
  Hyperventilation
  Emboli
  Thrombosis
  Vasculitis
  Subarachnoid hemorrhage

Electrolyte and Acid-Base Abnormality
 Na
 Ca
 K
 Mg
 pH

ENDOCRINE CAUSES

Pancreatic
 Hypoglycemia
  Exogenous
  Endogenous
 Hyperglycemia
  Ketotic
  Nonketotic

Pituitary and Adrenal
 Addison's disease
 Cushing's disease

Parathyroid
 Hypoparathyroid
 Hyperparathyroid

Thyroid   (hypothyroidism)

TOXINS, ENDOGENOUS

Uremia
Hepatic Coma
CO_2 Narcosis
Porphyria

TOXINS, EXOGENOUS

Barbiturates
Bromides
Tranquilizers
Alcohols
Opiates
Anticholinergics
Heavy Metals

DEFICIENCY

Thiamine
Niacin
Pyridoxine
Vitamin B_{12}

TABLE 5

Structural Causes of Coma

INFECTION

Abscess
  Intracerebral
  Subdural empyema
  Epidural empyema
Meningitis
Encephalitis

TRAUMA

Subdural Hematoma
  Chronic
  Acute
Epidural Hematoma
Intracerebral Hematoma
Contusion and Laceration
Cerebral Edema

TUMOR

Cerebral
  Intra-axial
    Glioma
    Ependymoma
    Metastatic
  Extra-axial
    Meningioma
    Metastatic
    Other

Posterior Fossa
  Intra-axial
    Hemangioblastoma
    Medulloblastoma
    Ependymoma
    Metastatic
  Extra-axial
    Meningioma
    Neuroma
    Other

TABLE 5 (CONT.)

Structural Causes of Coma

VASCULAR
Intracerebral Hemorrhage
  Putamen
  Thalamus
  Pons
  Cerebellum

Aneurysm
  Anterior communicating
  Posterior communicating
  Middle cerebral artery
  Other

Thrombosis and Embolus
  Internal carotid
  Anterior cerebral
  Middle cerebral
  Posterior cerebral
  Basilar
  Vertebral

AV-Malformation

6
Behavior Disorders

DEMENTIA

Dementia is a common symptom of frequently undiagnosed but treatable disorders. Although dementias are more than memory disorders, we attempt to localize a defect of memory anatomically by specific bedside tests. Thus immediate recall is tested by digit span (normals can immediately recall 7 ± 2 digits forward); recent memory is tested by recall of three objects (eg, house, boat, umbrella) after 3 to 5 minutes of distraction; remote memory is tested by fund of information. A frontal lobe memory disorder is much more difficult to test, but it is characterized by moment-to-moment fluctuations in testing other memory modalities, particularly immediate and recent. This is in large part because of frontal lobe hypokinesia with slowed responses and because of defective arousal. The probable executive control of attention arousal for the frontal lobes is mediated via strong connections from dorsolateral and cingulate areas to the mesencephalic reticular formation. Thus the patient will not have decreased consciousness (tonic arousal defect) and inability to receive any sensory input, as someone with bilateral mesencephalic reticular formation lesions might, but will have a greater problem with hypokinesia and mutism, with fluctuating memory tests because of disordered phasic arousal. Thus many of these patients can perform better if the external stimulus is increased in intensity. Orbitofrontal damage may give many of these patients inappropriate jocularity because of amygdaloid connections.

The specific sites and mechanisms of memory are little understood, but we have attempted to place these in a scheme to help distinguish these disorders clinically and provide a differential diagnosis and a guide to appropriate evaluation. Table 1 defines the various forms of memory disturbances. Table 2 classifies etiologies according to the type of memory disturbance they produce. Table 3 outlines the laboratory evaluation of dementia. Every patient with dementia should be completely evaluated by these tests to rule out a treatable dementia.

APHASIAS AND RELATED DISTURBANCES

Aphasias

Aphasia is a disturbance of language that is most frequently seen with left hemispheric lesions. Although aphasia can be seen with subcortical disease, it most frequently occurs with cortical disease. Examination of the aphasic patient not only helps the clinician assess his patient's abilities and disabilities but also helps localize the lesion. Examination of an aphasic patient should include the following: (1) listening to spontaneous speech and noting whether it is fluent or nonfluent and if it is paraphasic; (2) testing comprehension for spoken and printed language (reading); (3) testing ability to repeat sentences (eg, "The President lives in Washington."); (4) testing ability to name items; (5) testing ability to write. Based on these five tests, aphasics can be classified in one of several syndromes (Table 4). Aphasic disorders are usually caused by the same diseases that can cause a hemiparesis (see Chapter 2, Table 3), however, certain degenerative diseases are unusual causes of aphasia. Certain diseases that do not produce weakness may produce aphasia (ie, Alzheimer's disease and Pick's disease).

Apraxias

Apraxias are disturbances of motor function that are not caused by elemental weakness or by lack of comprehension. To ascertain whether a patient has apraxia, the clinician should do the following tests: (1) motor performance to command (ie, "Show me how you would open a door with a key."); (2) motor performance to imitation (ie, "Do what I do." Examiner pantomimes using a hammer.) and testing motor performance with actual objects.

There are at least two forms of apraxia. Although patients with idiomotor apraxia comprehend the examiner and have good strength (if patient has weakness of the right arm, test the left arm), they cannot perform correctly to either command or imitation; but this often improves somewhat with the actual object. Patients with ideational apraxia cannot perform to command but can imitate and use actual objects faultlessly. In another form of ideational apraxia, patients can imitate and perform to command but cannot use the actual object.

Ideomotor apraxia of the left hand but not the right can be caused by callosal lesions (infarctions of anterior cerebral artery, callosal and pericallosal tumors, and iatrogenicity); otherwise, ideomotor apraxia can be caused by hemispheric lesions similar to those seen with aphasia. Ideational apraxia (where the patient cannot perform to command) is seen with parietal lesions.

Gerstmann's Syndrome

Gerstmann's syndrome encompasses the following: (1) acalculia, a decreased ability to calculate; (2) finger agnosia, a decrease in the ability to name fingers; (3) right–left confusion, an inability to distinguish right from left on own or examiner's body; (4) agraphia, a decrease in the ability to write. Although agraphia can accompany aphasia, it may also appear with acalculia, finger agnosia, and right–left confusion as Gerstmann's syndrome, suggesting dominant parietal dysfunction. The cause of the parietal dysfunction is similar to the cause of aphasia.

Alexia

Alexia is defined as a defect in reading comprehension. There are two major types: alexia with agraphia and alexia without agraphia. Stroke is the most frequent etiology. Alexia without agraphia is caused by infarction in the distribution of the posterior cerebral artery, and alexia with agraphia is usually associated with dominant parietal infarction (middle cerebral artery). Both syndromes, however, may be caused by the same diseases that cause aphasia.

Constructional Apraxia

The most simple test for constructional apraxia is to ask the patient to draw a cube. Inability to draw a cube can derive from either right or left parietal dysfunction and is caused by the same diseases that produces aphasia.

Right Hemispheric Behavior Syndromes

The right hemispheric behavior syndromes include the following: (1) prosopagnosia, an inability to recognize familiar faces; (2) dressing apraxia, a loss of the ability to get dressed; (3) loss of depth perception; (4) spatial disorientation, in the absence of verbal clues, a defect in finding one's way around a familiar place or finding geographic locations on a map; (5) affective disorders (6) amusia, difficulty in recognizing known melodies. Almost all the above syndromes are seen from right parietal dysfunction. Again, the underlying diseases are usually the same as those that cause aphasia.

Agnosias

Agnosia is an inability to name or demonstrate the correct use of any object in spite of having intact primary sensation and language. There are two types of agnosias: (1) In associative agnosia the patient cannot name a stimulus but can replicate it or match it to a sample. The lesion that produces this disconnects the sensory association area from the inferior parietal lobe language areas. (2) In apperceptive agnosia the patient cannot replicate or match the stimulus to sample. In visual agnosia there is a defect in the association area, where, as in somesthetic agnosia and auditory agnosia, the defect may be in the cortical primary area. Etiologies of agnosia and aphasia are similar.

TABLE 1

Types of Memory Disorders

SIGNS AND SYMPTOMS	IMMEDIATE RECALL	RECENT MEMORY	REMOTE MEMORY	FRONTAL LOBE
Anatomic site of dysfunction	Reticular activating system language areas	Limbic system, especially hippocampus, mamillary bodies, fornix, and medial dorsal thalmus	Association cortex	Dorsolateral (frontal lobe), cingulate gyrus, orbitofrontal
Capacity	Limited	Limited	Not limited	Limited by input and time to recall
Neurochemical basis	Neurotransmitters	RNA; perhaps synthesis controlled by acetylcholine or serotonin or both	Protein molecules	Neurotransmitters
Distraction	Labile	Stable	Stable	Stable, if successfully aroused
Electroconvulsive therapy	Labile	Labile	Stable	Labile
Information loss	Decay with distraction	Displacement	Relearning, defective retrieval, engram destruction	Displacement
Clinical test	Digit span; Wechsler logical memory immediate	Wechsler delayed logical memory test; recall after distraction, eg, three objects after 3 minutes with interpolated activity	Performance on previously learned tasks; general information	History is most important*

*A frontal lobe memory defect is characterized by inattention (inability to create a stable intention to remember) and perseveration (pathologic inertia).

TABLE 2
Etiology of Dementias

	IMMEDIATE	FRONTAL	RECENT	REMOTE
Intoxicants	CNS depressants			
Infections	Acute meningitis or encephalitis, or both	General paralysis of the insane Abscess	Herpes simplex	Jakob-Creutzfeld disease Abscess
Metabolic encephalopathies	Hepatic, uremic hypercalcemic, increased CO_2, increased or decreased sodium, hypothyroidism, vitamin deficiencies (B_{12}, folate, niacin)	Marchiafava-Bignami disease	Anoxia, hypoglycemia, carbon monoxide, Korsakoff's amnesic dementia, hyperlipidemia	
Trauma	Acute, concussion, chronic subdural	Orbitofrontal, frontopolar damage	Bilateral temporal lobectomy, mesial temporal lobe damage, subdural with temporal lobe herniation	Parietal lobe contusions and lacerations
Increased intracranial pressure	Hypertensive encephalopathy, mass lesions, obstructive hydrocephalus	Obstructive hydrocephalus, communicating hydrocephalus (pressure normal or low)	Temporal lob herniation	
Tumors	Producing increased intracranial pressure	Frontal lobe, e.g., meningiomas, "butterfly" gliomas	Tumors of IIIrd ventricle, Pituitary tumor	Large gliomas or multiple metastases
Vascular		Arteriosclerosis, vasculitis, anterior communicating aneurysm	Posterior cerebral artery ischemia (transient global amnesia)	Lacunar state Vasculitis
Degenerative		Progressive supranuclear palsy of Steele-Richardson-Olzewski; Probably late multiple sclerosis	Alzheimer's disease Pick's disease	Alzheimer's disease Pick's disease

TABLE 3

Laboratory Evaluation of Dementia

REQUIRED STUDIES
Complete blood count
FTA
Serum lipids
Electrolytes (sodium, potassium, chloride, carbon dioxide)
Blood gases if indicated
Calcium, phosphate
Vitamin B_{12} (screen with free gastric acid)
Folate
Liver functions
Renal function (blood urea nitrogen, creatinine)
Thyroid function (protein-bound iodine [PBI], thyroxine [T_4])
Chest x-ray
Skull x-ray
CAT scan
Electroencephalogram
Echoencephalogram if available
Lumbar puncture
  Pressure
  Cells and differential
  Protein electrophoresis if indicated (syphilis)
  Glucose with concomitant blood glucose
  VDRL test
  Gram stain, acid-fast bacillus stain, India ink stain if indicated
  Cultures for bacteria, acid-fast bacillus, fungus if indicated

ADDITIONAL STUDIES THAT MAY BE REQUIRED
Metastatic survey
Radioiodinated serum albumin cisternography
Pneumoencephalography or ventriculography
Brain biopsy
Cerebral angiography
Acute and convalescent viral antibody titers
Acute and convalescent fungal antibody titers

TABLE 4

Aphasic Disorders

TYPE	COMPRE-HENSION (SPOKEN)	COMPRE-HENSION (WRITTEN)	REPETITION	NAMING	SPONTANEOUS SPEECH	LESION SITE AND UNDERLYING MECHANISM
Pure word deafness	Poor	Normal	Poor	Normal	Normal	Bilateral destruction of primary auditory areas or disconnection of auditory areas from Wernicke's area
Wernicke's aphasia	Poor	Poor	Poor	Poor	Fluent, paraphasic jargon, logorrhea	Lesion in Wernicke's area (posterior portion of superior temporary gyrus); Wernicke's area is important in phonemic processing
Transcortical aphasia (sensory and mixed)	Poor	May read aloud without comprehension	Normal with echolalia	Poor	In sensory; paraphasic; in mixed, nonfluent	Destruction of semantic areas (? parietal lobes) or disconnection between phonemic area (Wernicke's area) and remainder of brain
Anomic aphasia	Good	May be impaired	Normal	Poor	Circumlocations and paraphasia	Lesion may be remote from speech area or in angular gyrus; ? disconnection of semantic area from phonemic area, but phonemic area has access to semantic area

TABLE 4 (CONT.)

Aphasic Disorders

TYPE	COMPREHENSION (SPOKEN)	COMPREHENSION (WRITTEN)	REPETION	NAMING	SPONTANEOUS SPEECH	LESION SITE AND UNDERLYING MECHANISM
Mixed transcortical aphasia with intact naming	Poor	May read aloud without comprehension	Normal with echolalia	Good	Nonfluent	? disconnection of phonemic area from semantic area, but semantic area has access to phonemic area
Conduction aphasia	Good	May be impaired	Poor	Good or poor	Fluent to mild dysfluent; paraphasic	Lesion may be in either arcuate gyrus or Wernicke's area; in former, lesion disconnects Wernicke's area from Broca's area; in latter case, right hemisphere mediates language
Broca's aphasia	Good	Good or impaired	Poor	Poor	Nonfluent, agrammatic	Broca's area (third frontal convolution)
Aphemia	Normal	Normal	Poor	Poor	Mute; writing normal	? disconnection between Broca's area and primary motor areas
Transcortical motor aphasia	Normal	Normal	Normal		Nonfluent	Left medial frontal lobe or dorsolateral frontal lobe superior to Broca's area; ? akinesia of speech

7
Autonomic Disorders

Occasionally the physician may see a patient who complains of a disorder of his autonomic nervous system. There are many symptoms the patient may present with (ie, orthostatic hypotension, abnormal sweating, disorders of temperature regulation). These diseases are outlined in Table 1.

Obstructive disease is the most common cause of micturition disturbances; however, when there is no source of obstruction or when there is incontinence, a neurogenic bladder may be producing the voiding difficulty. In attempting to learn the nature of the neurogenic bladder, a thorough neurologic examination must be performed to determine if there is evidence for hemispheric disease or cord disease. A neurogenic bladder may also be caused by lower motor neuron disease. Therefore one should examine rectal tone, anal wink, bulbocavernosus reflex, strength of foot plantar flexors, and ankle jerks. Perianal sensation should also be checked. Frequently, a cystometrogram may also be helpful in defining the nature of the neurogenic bladder. The differential diagnosis of neurogenic bladder is given in Table 2. The sites of the different lesions that produce a neurogenic bladder can be found in Figure 5.

TABLE 1

Autonomic Disorders

DISEASE	ORTHOSTATIC HYPOTENSION	HYPERTENSION	DISORDERS OF SWEATING	DISORDERS OF TEMPERATURE REGULATION	OTHER DISORDERS
Old age and cerebrovascular disease	May be present			May be present	May be produced by debility rather than vascular disease
Spinal cord lesion	May be present	May be present	May be present	May be present	Lesion usually has to be higher than T-6; hypertension may be associated with bradycardia and vasodilation proximal to lesion (see Chapter 2)
Acute polyneuropathy (Guillain-Barré porphyria)	May be present	May be present	May be present	May be present	May also be associated with cardiac abnormalities
Chronic polyneuropathy	May be present, especially with diabetic neuropathy		May be present		See Chapter 2
Parkinson's disease	May be present		May be present	May be present	L-dopa may make postural hypotension worse; therefore dopa decarboxylase inhibitor should be used
Tabes dorsalis	May be present				
Intracranial hypertension		May be present			Associated with bradycardia and other signs of increased intracranial pressure

Idiopathic orthostatic hypotension	Present		May be present	Seen most frequently in men; may be associated with impotence, sphincter dysfunction
Holmes-Adie syndrome	May be present		May be present	Disorder of pupil (tonic pupil)
Hypothalamic lesion		May be present	May be present	Symptoms may be intermittent, diencephalic epilepsy
Familial dysautonomia (Riley-Day syndrome)	May be present	May be present	May be present	Autosomal recessive disease in Jews; other symptoms include retardation, emotional disorders, insensitivity to pain, abnormal lacrimation
Tetanus		May be present	May be present	
Anorexia nervosa	May be present			
Deficient catecholamine release	Present			Most patients with idiopathic orthostatic hypotension have normal catecholamines
Drugs	Chlorpromazine, meprobamate, barbiturates, MAO inhibitors, antihypertensives	MAO inhibitors and ergots, tyramine, noradreanalin and other sympathomimetic drugs	Anticholinesterases	Anesthesia (malignant hypertension), tricyclic antidepressants, MAO inhibitors, chlorpromazine

TABLE 2
Differential Diagnosis of Neurogenic Bladder

TYPE OF BLADDER	NATURE OF DEFECT	LOCATION OF LESION*	SYMPTOMS	CYSTOMETRO-GRAM	NEUROLOGIC SIGNS THAT MAY BE ASSOCIATED	TREATMENT†
Uninhibited	Corticoregulatory	Cortical, subcortical, cord	Hesitancy, frequency, urgency, and finally urgency incontinence	Sensation normal; voiding contraction uncontrolled	Dementia (see Chapter 6, Table 2), frontal lobe signs (grasp, suck, paratonia), bilateral pyramidal signs	Treat infection; treat underlying neurologic disease; atropine, but must watch for retention
Reflex	Corticoregulatory and afferent	Cord	May not start or stop micturition; no sensation; may be associated with bradycardia and hypertension	No sensation; otherwise like the above	Cord lesions (see Chapter 2, Table 5)	Treat underlying disease and infection; bladder training; may need urologic surgical procedures
Autonomous	Both afferent and efferent limbs of reflex arch	Cauda equina, conus medullaris, roots	Cannot void except with overflow incontinence and with Crede maneuver	No sensation; no voluntary or involuntary contractions	Absent anal wink; bulbocavernosus, rectal tone and perianal sensation; may also have decreased ankle jerk and lower extremity weakness	Treat underlying disease and infection; Crede maneuver may not be sufficient, and urologic procedures may be needed

Sensory paralytic	Interruption of afferents	Afferent limb	Because patient does not feel full bladder, the bladder may become distended and have decreased force of stream	Abnormal sensation, increased capacity, increased residual	Absent anal wink; bulbocavernosus and decreased perianal sensation; may be seen with tabes dorsalis, pernicious anemia, diabetes, syringomyelia	Urecholine and training for frequent urination
Motor paralytic	Lower motor neuron	Lower motor neuron	Painful distended bladder; unable to void; appears as obstructive uropathy	Normal sensation; no contractions	Absent anal wink, bulbocavernosus, and rectal tone	If partial, may be treated with urecholine; if complete, need urologic procedures

*See Figure 5.
†For details, consult a urology text.

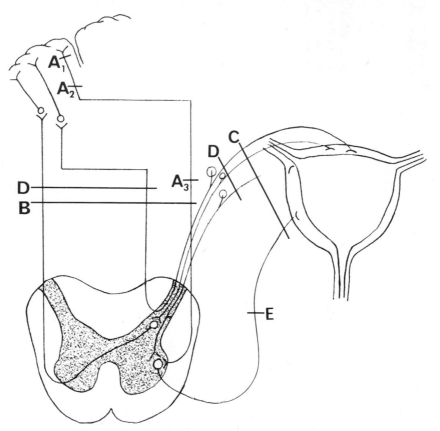

FIG. 5. Sites of lesions in neurogenic bladder. **A.** *Uninhibited bladder* (cortex, subcortical, cord)   **B.** *Reflex neurogenic bladder* (cord or large brain lesions)   **C.** *Autonomous bladder* (conus or cauda, or motor and/or sensory roots). **D.** *Sensory paralytic bladder* (sensory roots or afferent tracts). **E.** *Motor paralytic bladder* (motor root and/or nerve).

All lesions that cause neurogenic bladder are bilateral.

8
Increased Intracranial Pressure

All patients with complaints referable to the head are considered potentially to be suffering from increased intracranial pressure. Headache, tinnitus, dizziness, nausea, vomiting, decreased alertness, and blurred or double vision are all nonspecific symptoms that may or may not be present in a specific patient. The so-called characteristic early morning traction headache accompanied by nausea and vomiting that is seen in the patient with brain tumor is more often than not absent. Basically, a history of progressive disturbance in which the above constellation of symptoms occurs should alert the physician to any process giving rise to increased pressure.

Signs of increased intracranial pressure include papilledema and nonlocalizing cranial nerve palsies (usually cranial nerve VI). The appearance of focal neurologic signs such as hemiparesis implies a localized mass process. Other features such as seizures, obtundation, and evidence of meningeal irritation associated with a history of fever, trauma, hypertension, etc, define the nature of the disease process (Table 1).

Resolution of the problem assumes a degree of urgency based on certain important considerations. Increasing intracranial pressure, as caused by a lateralized mass, will often lead to a shift of cerebral tissue, resulting in herniation through fixed dural connections or the foramen magnum. Com-

129

pression of the third cranial nerve (dilated fixed pupil) by herniated tissue through the tentorial notch is an emergency situation. Impending compression of the brainstem is heralded by a slowing of the pulse and increasing systemic blood pressure (Cushing effect).

Increased intracranial pressure caused by a supratentorial mass process may evolve slowly, and a progression of neurologic reflex phenomena will provide guideposts for the astute physician regarding the so-called rostral-caudal dysfunction. Early diencephalic compression by a mass effect is usually heralded by a depression in the state of consciousness accompanied by minor irregularities in the breathing pattern. Small, poorly reactive pupils and the emergence of bilateral upper motor neuron dysfunction (increased tone, hyperreflexia, Babinski signs) are also seen. With the progression of the pressure effect on the diencephalon, the breathing pattern becomes more irregular (Cheyne-Stokes in type); obtundation is evident, and decorticate motor posturing is assumed. Midbrain or upper brainstem compression then ensues, and the breathing may be a sustained type of hyperventilation; brainstem pupillary and oculomotor reflex responses become inadequate (caloric stimulation, ciliospinal reflex, doll's-head reaction, response to light stimulus), and decerebrate posturing of the trunk and extremities is noted. This stage passes into the irreversible medullary compression picture characterized by irregular shallow breathing, loss of all brainstem reflexes, and generalized flaccidity.

In less urgent situations, as gauged by the patient's state of alertness, a sequential series of diagnostic studies may be carried out. These are listed with their expected findings for disease categories known to cause increased intracranial pressure (Table 2).

A special comment should be made regarding the importance of the decision for lumbar puncture. In essence, if the procedure will provide critical information that will define the illness and lead to specific therapy, such as in the case of the infant who suffers from acute bacterial meningitis, then the lumbar puncture is justified. In the presence of a neoplasm, a lumbar puncture may confirm the pressure as being increased and the spinal fluid protein as being elevated, but the procedure adds nothing specific to the diagnosis and entails a major risk by predisposing to the problem of herniation and brainstem compression.

Other studies to be performed if time permits include skull x-rays, chest x-ray, brain scan, electroencephalogram, computerized tomography, and the invasive studies arteriography and air encephalography. Increased intracranial pressure, particularly if it is long-standing, causes skull x-ray changes, including erosion of the dorsum sellae and the anterior and posterior clinoids, and in time the so-called beaten-silver appearance reflecting the gyral pattern under pressure. In the presence of a mass, the pineal, if calcified, will be shifted away from the midline. Furthermore, calcium may be seen in tumors; the inner table of the skull may be thickened (meningioma) or eroded (metastatic lesion). In the child, increased pressure is manifested by widening of the sutures.

TABLE 1

Diseases That May Produce Increased Intracranial Pressure: Clinical Features

CONDITION	ONSET	MISCELLANEOUS SYMPTOMS AND SIGNS	COURSE AND COMMENT	TREATMENT
Trauma				
Cerebral swelling	Abrupt	Obtundation, focal neurologic signs corresponding to area of insult (eg, hemiparesis, aphasia, blindness) ± seizures	Maximum swelling may occur 24 to 48 hours after trauma	Supportive; maintain breathing, fluids; use of steroids controversial
Subdural hematoma	Abrupt or insidiously evolving	If slowly evolving, headache, progressive obtundation; if unilateral hematoma, lateralized signs of motor impairment; if rapid, depression of mental function	Progressively worsening clinical picture; may or may not see skull fracture	Surgical evacuation
Epidural hematoma	Abrupt	Rapidly evolving picture of unilateral hemisphere and brainstem compression with coma	Rapid progression within minutes to hours; skull fracture across middle meningeal artery	Immediate surgical evacuation and ligation of bleeding artery
Sagittal sinus thrombosis	Slowly progressive if localized; rapid if there is cortical vein thrombosis as well	If limited to sagittal sinus, general complaints of increased intracranial pressure; if cortical veins become thrombosed, focal signs and seizures become apparent	Often see fracture across sagittal sinus	Supportive treatment to control seizures and increased intracranial pressure; anticoagulants contraindicated because of bleeding
Leptomeningeal cyst	Progressive over months or years	Focal signs of cerebral compression caused by mass effect of ball-valve extradural arachnoid cyst	Skull x-rays reveal defect in inner table of skull	Simple surgical repair of cyst

Neoplasm

	Course	Clinical features	Comments	Treatment
Primary intracranial (glioma, oligodendroglioma, ependymoma, meningioma, glioblastoma, medulloblastoma, neuroma, other)	Insidiously progressive for months, or rapidly evolving if ventricular obstruction or hemorrhage within neoplasm occurs	If unilateral, progressive signs of focal impairment concomitant with nonspecific features of increased pressure; if midline, truncal instability and features of increased pressure occur	Benign neoplasm may exist in noncritical areas for years without detection; seizures in adults without apparent exogenous cause should alert examiner to existence of neoplasm	Surgical removal if possible; certain tumors are radiosensitive; chemotherapeutic approach palliative
Metastatic (lung, breast, kidney, melanoma, other)	Usually rapidly progressive, often heralded by seizures	Associated cerebral edema causes significant focal signs and symptoms of increased pressure	Great probability of more than one metastatic brain lesion if primary is lung; kidney lesion may be isolated	Corticosteroid treatment effective in ameliorating edema effect; surgical treatment effective if single metastasis thought to exist (based on nature of primary)
Meningeal neoplasm (metastases, leukemia)	Progressive development of intracranial pressure caused by obstruction of CSF flow (and possibly obstruction of venous return)	Head pain and cranial nerve signs often seen, caused by infiltration at base	Increased pressure may fluctuate during early phase of illness	Radiation, corticosteroids; systemic and intrathecal chemotherapy

Infection

Abscess

	Course	Clinical features	Comments	Treatment
Intracerebral	Subacute course, weeks	Focal signs and seizures are common; fever or subnormal temperature	Once pressure within abscess reaches significant level, then intraventricular rupture causes death	Treatment with antibiotics and surgical removal; search and treatment of primary infection in lung, sinus, etc
Subdural or epidural empyema	Very rapidly progressive	Secondary vasculitis affecting cortical veins commonly causes seizures early; related to sinusitis or osteomyelitis	Venous occlusion as well as mass effect causes rapid increase in intracranial pressure	Surgical evacuation urgent; treat primary source

TABLE 1 (CONT.)

Diseases That May Produce Increased Intracranial Pressure: Clinical Features

CONDITION	ONSET	MISCELLANEOUS SYMPTOMS AND SIGNS	COURSE AND COMMENT	TREATMENT
Mycotic aneurysm	Subacute	Cardiac disease predisposes to acute or subacute endocarditis; seizures, septic course	Features of generalized sepsis; hemorrhage, anemia, weight loss, etc	Antibiotics after blood culture
Bacterial meningitis Common (pneumococcus, heningococcus, Haemophilus influenzae)	Rapid and fulminating	Features of meningeal irritability, fever, seizures	Treatment urgent, within hours, before irreversible damage; subdural effusion of empyema must be considered if antibiotics ineffective	Culture of CSF and blood before treatment with antibiotics
Uncommon (Streptococcus, Staphylococcus, Listeria, Escherichia coli, Pseudomonas)	Subacute	In association with other chronic processes in newborn or related to indolent source of infection; evidence of meningeal irritation slow to appear	Diagnosis may be suspected on basis of only vague symptoms, eg, lethargy, poor feeding, etc	Culture and appropriate antibiotic therapy
Tuberculous meningitis	Subacute	Features of systemic infection common with superimposed process of meningeal irritation	Focal signs may appear early as a result of vascular occlusion; complications include subdural effusion and hydrocephalus	Culture and appropriate chemotherapy

Disease	Onset	Clinical features	Course	Treatment
Viral meningitis (infectious mononucleosis, echovirus, coxsackie virus, mumps, acute lymphocytic meningitis, herpes simplex)	Acute	Preexisting systemic signs and symptoms (respiratory, gastrointestinal) followed by signs of meningeal irritation	Gradual resolution of signs and symptoms within days; however, complete recovery usually in weeks	Supportive care
Viral encephalitis (mumps, herpes simplex, coxsackie B, inclusion body; rabies, Epstein-Barr virus, infectious mononucleosis, arthropod-borne virus, measles, etc)	Acute	Features of encephalopathy; headache, disorientation, lethargy, seizures; may have focal signs (herpes simplex, temporal lobe)	As above	Supportive care
Fungus meningitis (cryptococcosis, coccidioidomycosis, actinomycosis, aspergillosis, candidiasis, histoplasmosis, nocardiosis)	Subacute	Often non specific symptoms of headache with vague signs of meningeal irritation	Chronic systemic diseases often predispose (eg, diabetes); despite treatment, infection may recur or relapse	Amphotericin, 5-fluocytosine
Parasitic infestation (amebic meningoencephalitis, malaria, visceral larva migrans, Echinococcus)	Acute or chronic	May be acute and fulminating (amebic meningoencephalitis), or may be chronic and present as a mass process (echinococcosis); focal and generalized signs may be present	Unremitting course, depending on nature of parasite	Treatment may be chemotherapy or surgery

TABLE 1 (CONT.)

Diseases That May Produce Increased Intracranial Pressure: Clinical Features

CONDITION	ONSET	MISCELLANEOUS SYMPTOMS AND SIGNS	COURSE AND COMMENT	TREATMENT
Hydrocephalus				
Congenital (aqueductal stenosis and deformity, Arnold-Chiari malformation, Klippel-Feil deformity, posterior fossa cyst, craniosynostosis, Dandy-Walker syndrome, achondroplasia, basilar impression, cranioskeletal dysplasia)	Subacute and progressive	Associated cranial or spinal abnormalities to be sought at same time specific hydrocephalic problem (cyst, aqueductal stenosis, etc) is defined	Search for additional malformations and recognition of multiple defects	Surgical diversion of fluid from obstructed ventricle or removal of obstructing process
Acquired Postinfectious (toxoplasmosis, cytomegalic inclusion disease, bacterial meningitis, syphilis)	Subacute and progressive	Search for primary cause to give prognostic guidance	Obstruction of flow of fluid at base of brain or aqueduct	As above, unless cause is related to a degenerative process, eg, mucopolysaccharidosis
Posthemorrhagic Mucopolysaccharidosis				

Vascular Disease

	Onset	Signs	Treatment
Intracerebral hemorrhage (contributory factors: hypertension, clotting mechanism deficiencies, hemophilia, thrombotic thrombocytopenia, thrombocytopenia, vascular malformation)	Sudden	Signs of neurologic impairment related to site of hemorrhage and surrounding swelling; if cerebellar hemorrhage, increased pressure develops rapidly as a result of fourth ventricle obstruction	Diagnosis as to cause essential, since treatment may prevent worsening (eg, antihypertensive agents, antihemophilic globulin)	In selected instances, surgical evacuation critical, eg, hemorrhage from vascular malformation; hypertensive hemorrhage usually surgically untreatable, unless in cerebellum; control of bleeding diathesis or hypertension
Subarachnoid hemorrhage	Sudden	Severe headache plus signs of meningeal irritation	In alert nonhypertensive patient, cerebral arteriography may define accessible lesion for surgical removal; rebleeding potential for aneurysm	Antihypertensive therapy for patient with hypertension, antifidrinolytic agents, and in selected patients surgical treatment of aneurysm
Hypertensive encephalopathy	Sudden	Headache precedes signs of diffuse encephalopathy (seizures, confusion, etc); focal signs identify stroke process supervening	Need to control hypertension rapidly to prevent further insult	Antihypertensive and supportive therapy (ie, anticonvulsants)
Large stroke	Sudden	Appearance of increased intracranial pressure after 2–3 days; until then, focal signs corresponding to infarcted area	Prognosis for recovery of function in large stroke poor	Supportive therapy; steroids may reduce swelling and preserve life, but deficit is profound
Vasculitis	Sudden	Similar to hypertensive encephalopathy	Multiple focal areas of deficit	Corticosteroids

TABLE 1 (CONT.)

Diseases That May Produce Increased Intracranial Pressure: Clinical Features

CONDITION	ONSET	MISCELLANEOUS SYMPTOMS AND SIGNS	COURSE AND COMMENT	TREATMENT
Venous thrombosis (contributory factors: dehydration, postpartum state, oral contraceptives, polycythemia)	Sudden	Increased intracranial pressure occurs with seizures and focal neurologic signs	Rapidly progressive course, unless cause corrected, and collaterals are adequate	Anticoagulation contraindicated because of bleeding; supportive care and anticonvulsants
Toxic and Metabolic Disease				
Heavy-metal poisoning (lead, thallium, arsenic)	Subacute and progressive or rapid	General features of encephalopathy accompanying increased intracranial pressure (seizures, obtundation, etc)	Index of suspicion needed to make diagnosis (anemia, hair loss, polyneuropathy, etc)	Supportive measures, chelating agents, BAL
Reye's syndrome	Acute, rapidly progressive	Acute encephalopathy (agitation, seizures, progressing to coma)	Associated features of hepatic failure	Dialysis, supportive measures, citrulline or arginine nifusions controversial
Benign intracranial hypertension Contributory causes or associated factors:	Subacute	Nonspecific signs of increased intracranial pressure and headache; visual impairment major concern	Associated condition to be sought	Specific treatment, depending on provoking factors; supportive measures, serial lumbar punctures

Intracranial venous
drainage obstruc-
tion; mastoiditis
and lateral (sigmoid)
sinus obstruction,
extracerebral mass
lesions, congenital
atresia or stenosis
of venous sinuses,
head trauma, cryo-
fibrinogenemia, poly-
cythemia vera,
paranasal sinus and
pharyngeal infec-
tions, intrathoracic
mass lesions and
postsurgical ob-
struction of
venous return

Endocrine dys-
function:
pregnancy, menarche,
marked menstrual
irregularities,
oral contraceptives,
obesity, withdrawal
of corticosteroid
therapy, Addison's
disease, hypopara-
thyroidism

139

TABLE 1 (CONT.)

Diseases That May Produce Increased Intracranial Pressure: Clinical Features

CONDITION	ONSET	MISCELLANEOUS SYMPTOMS AND SIGNS	COURSE AND COMMENT	TREATMENT
Hematologic disorders: acute iron-deficiency anemia, pernicious anemia, thrombocytopenia, Wiscott-Aldrich syndrome				
Vitamin disorders: chronic hypervitaminosis A, acute hypervitaminosis A, hypovitaminosis A				
Drug reactions: tetracycline, gentamicin, nalidixic acid, sulfamethoxazole, penicillin, prophylactic antisera				
Miscellaneous: deprivation dwarfism, galactokinase deficiency, Sydenham's chorea, roseola infantum, hypophosphatasia				

			Contributory process sought	
Fluid and electrolyte disturbances (increased ADH secretion, renal disease, iatrogenic fluid overload)	Subacute	Encephalopathy (confusion, disorientation, obtundation seizures)		Regulation of fluid and electrolyte abnormality
Ketoacidosis (diabetes mellitus)	Subacute	Encephalopathy	Regulation of diabetic imbalance	Insulin, fluids
Miscellaneous Disease				
Demyelinating disease	Subacute as well as rapidly progressive	Appearance of focal, then generalized, features of encephalopathy	History of previous episodes of neurologic impairment suggest demyelination	High-dose corticosteroids
Granulomatous disease (sarcoidosis, histiocytosis)	Insidious, fluctuating	Signs of meningeal irritation, focal cranial nerve impairment	Arachnoid adhesions obstruct spinal fluid passage and cause cranial nerve signs	Corticosteroids
Paget's disease	Slowly evolving	Encroachment on cranial foramina may lead to cranial nerve deficits	Progressive bone changes in skull lead to obstruction of free access of CSF	Surgical decompression
Increased CSF protein (spinal cord tumor, post-infectious polyneuropathy)	Slowly evolving	Neurologic impairment reflected in basic process (cord tumor, polyneuropathy)	Increased CSF protein ostensibly obstructs egress of fluid through arachnoid granulation	Treatment of basic process causing increased protein
Post status epilepticus, post anoxia	Rapid	Encephalopathic features (depression of consciousness, seizures, possible focal signs)	Emergence of increased intracranial pressure about 2–3 days after anoxic insult	Control of status, supportive measures; effect of corticosteroids controversial

TABLE 1 (CONT.)

Diseases That May Produce Increased Intracranial Pressure: Clinical Features

CONDITION	ONSET	MISCELLANEOUS SYMPTOMS AND SIGNS	COURSE AND COMMENT	TREATMENT
Cardiopulmonary disease (chronic pulmonary disease, alveolar hypoventilation, congestive heart failure)	Subacute, progressive	Encephalopathy (altered consciousness, seizures)	Hypercarbia leads to intracranial vasodilatation and increased pressure; severe right heart failure may also cause impaired flow returning through superior vena cava	Treat underlying cardiopulmonary disease
Mediastinal disease	Subacute, progressive	Headache and other nonspecific signs and symptoms of increased pressure	Obstruction of venous return of intracranial blood	Surgery if obstruction can be removed; if mediastinitis, just supportive care until collateral channels open for venous drainage
Meningismus	Acute	Response to acute febrile state in infancy; bulging fontanelle	Presumably related to sudden shifts of osmolar content between blood and CSF	Treat underlying febrile problem

TABLE 2

Differential Diagnosis of Increased Intracranial Pressure: Laboratory Studies

CONDITION	SKULL X-RAY	ECHOENCEPHALOGRAM	BRAIN SCAN	EEG	COMPUTERIZED TOMOGRAPHY	CEREBRAL ARTERIOGRAM
Trauma						
Cerebral swelling	Fracture or negative	Midline if symmetric swelling	Negative	Diffuse slowing	Negative	Negative
Subdural hematoma	Often fracture, pineal shifted if unilateral	Shift if unilateral	Positive	Electrical depression over hematoma	Shift of lateral ventricles; mass	Displacement of vessels from skull
Epidural hematoma	Fracture usually across middle meningeal, artery, pineal shifted if unilateral	Shift if unilateral	Positive	Electrical depression over hematoma	Shift of lateral ventricles; mass	Displacement of vessels
Sagittal sinus thrombosis	Often fracture	Midline	Negative	Normal or diffuse slowing	Negative	Occlusion of sagittal sinus
Leptomeningeal cyst	Defect (old fracture)	Shift	Negative	Focal depression of electrical activity	Area of decreased tissue density	Displacement of vessels

TABLE 2 (CONT.)

Differential Diagnosis of Increased Intracranial Pressure: Laboratory Studies

CONDITION	SKULL X-RAY	CHEST X-RAY	BRAIN SCAN	EEG	COMPUTERIZED TOMOGRAPHY	CEREBRAL ARTERIOGRAM
Neoplasm						
Primary intracranial (glioblastoma, astrocytoma, oligodendrogioma, ependymoma, and others)	Calcified pineal may be shifted; dorsum sellae may be eroded; focal calcium deposits; inner table may be eroded or sclerotic	Negative	Positive	Focal abnormalities	Mass; ventricle shift eroded; focal	Mass
Metastatic (lung breast, kidney, melanoma, and others)	Same	Positive	Positive	Focal abnormalities	Masses; ventricle shift	Mass
Meningeal dissemination	Same	May be positive	Usually negative	May be diffusely slow	Negative	Vessel abnormality at base (CSF: carcinoma cells

TABLE 2 (CONT.)

Differential Diagnosis of Increased Intracranial Pressure: Laboratory Studies

CONDITION	SKULL X-RAY	CHEST X-RAY	BRAIN SCAN	EEG	COMPUTERIZED TOMOGRAPHY	ARTERIO-GRAM	LUMBAR PUNCTURE
Infection							
Abscess	Sinus may be clouded; dorsum sellae may be eroded	May reveal infiltration	Positive	Focal abnormalities	Positive	Mass	May show cells and increased protein
Bacterial meningitis	Sinus may be clouded	May reveal infiltration	Negative	Diffuse slowing	Negative	Negative	PMN pleocytosis; protein increased; sugar decreased; positive culture
Tuberculous meningitis	Negative	May reveal miliary infiltration or primary complex	Negative	Diffuse slowing	May reveal dilated ventricles	May reveal dilated ventricles	Mononuclear pleocytosis; protein increased; sugar decreased; positive culture
Viral meningitis	Negative	Negative	Negative	Negative	Negative	Negative	Mononuclear pleocytosis; protein increased; sugar normal; negative culture

TABLE 2 (CONT.)

CONDITION	SKULL X-RAY	CHEST X-RAY	BRAIN SCAN	EEG	COMPUTERIZED TOMOGRAPHY	ARTERIO-GRAM	LUMBAR PUNCTURE
Viral encephalitis	Negative	Negative	May be positive if herpes	May be focally slow if herpes	May reveal dilated ventricles or focal mass	May be positive if herpes	As in viral meningitis
Fungal meningitis	Dorsum sellae may be eroded	Negative	Negative	Diffuse slowing	May reveal dilated ventricles	May reveal dilated ventricles	Mononuclear pleocytosis; protein increased; sugar decreased; positive culture; India ink stain may be positive
Parasitic infestation	Dorsum sellae eroded	Negative	Positive	Focal or diffuse abnormalities	May reveal dilated ventricles or mass	Dilated ventricles or mass	Mononuclear pleocytosis; protein increased
Brucellosis	Negative	Negative	Negative	Diffuse slowing	Negative	Negative	RBCs; PMNs; mononuclear pleocytosis; increased protein

TABLE 2 (CONT.)

Differential Diagnosis of Increased Intracranial Pressure: Laboratory Studies

CONDITION	SKULL X-RAY	BRAIN SCAN	EEG	COMPUTERIZED TOMOGRAPHY
Hydrocephalus				
Congenital	If child, macrocranium, separated sutures; may see deformity at base	Negative	Negative	Enlarged ventricles
Acquired	Erosion of dorsum sellae	Negative	Dysrhythmia in presence of parenchymal damage	Enlarged ventricles

TABLE 2 (CONT.)

Differential Diagnosis of Increased Intracranial Pressure: Laboratory Studies

CONDITION	SKULL X-RAY	BRAIN SCAN	EEG	COMPUTERIZED TOMOGRAPHY	ARTERIOGRAM	LUMBAR PUNCTURE
Vascular Diseases						
Intracerebral hemorrhage	Pineal may be shifted	Positive (after 5 days)	Focal slowing	Mass	Mass	May see RBCs
Subarachnoid hemorrhage	Negative	Negative	Negative	Negative	Aneurysm	RBCs
Hypertensive encephalopathy	Negative	Negative	Diffuse slowing	Negative		Negative
Large stroke	Negative	Positive (after 5 days)	Focal slowing	Positive	Major vessel occlusion	Negative
Vasculitis	Negative	May be positive	Focal or diffuse abnormalities	Negative	Medium-size artery disease	RBCs
Intracranial venous thrombosis	Negative	May be positive	Focal or diffuse abnormalities	Negative	Various occlusion	RBCs

TABLE 2 (CONT.)

Differential Diagnosis of Increased Intracranial Pressure: Laboratory Studies

CONDITION	SKULL X-RAY	BRAIN SCAN	EEG	COMPUTERIZED TOMOGRAPHY	LUMBAR PUNCTURE
Toxic and Metabolic Disease					
Heavy-metal poisoning	Erosion of dorsum sellae, separation of sutures (child)	Negative	Diffuse slowing	Negative	Increased protein
Reye's syndrome	Negative	Negative	Diffuse slowing	Negative	Negative
Benign intracranial hypertension	Erosion of dorsum sellae	Negative	Negative	Negative	Negative
Fluid and electrolyte disturbances	Negative	Negative	Diffuse slowing	Negative	Negative (may be RBCs if hypermolar state)
Ketoacidosis (eg, diabetes)	Negative	Negative	Diffuse slowing	Negative	Negative; increased protein

149

TABLE 2 (CONT.)

Differential Diagnosis of Increased Intracranial Pressure: Laboratory Studies

CONDITION	SKULL X-RAY	CHEST X-RAY	BRAIN SCAN	EEG	LUMBAR PUNCTURE
Miscellaneous Diseases					
Degenerative disease (eg, Schilder's disease)	Negative	Negative	May be positive	Focal change	Increased gamma globulin
Granulomatous (eg, sarcoidosis)	May show erosion	May be positive	May be positive	Slowing possible	Pleocytosis (lymphocytosis); sugar may be depressed
Paget's disease	Bone changes	Negative	Negative	Negative	Negative
Cord mass, post infectious neuropathy	Eroded dorsum sellae	Negative	Negative	Negative	Markedly increased protein
Post status epilepticus, post anoxia	Negative	Negative	Negative	Diffuse slowing	Negative
Cardiopulmonary disease	Negative	Positive	Negative	Diffuse slowing	Negative
Mediastinal disease	May show eroded dorsum sellae	Positive	Negative	Negative	Negative
Meningismus	Negative	May reveal infiltrate	Negative	Negative	Negative

9
Cranial Nerve Dysfunction

ANATOMIC AND FUNCTIONAL RELATIONSHIPS

Recognition of cranial nerve abnormalities and an anatomic understanding of these abnormalities are necessary for localization. A brief outline of the locations, destinations, and functions of the cranial nerves is a prerequisite to recognition of dysfunction. These are outlined in Table 1.

CENTRAL VASOMOTOR AND RESPIRATORY DISORDERS

Respiratory centers are in the pons and medulla. These centers are under control of the orbitofrontal cortex and hypothalamus. The *inspiratory center* is in the medial reticular substance and the medial part of the lateral reticular substance of the medulla. The *expiratory center* is lateral and dorsal to the inspiratory center and is still in the medulla. Their responses may be to changes in hydrogen ions brought about through changes in carbon dioxide levels and sensed by structures in the roof of the medulla bathed by CSF of the fourth ventricle. The *pneumotaxic center* is in the upper pontine tegmentum; it inhibits respiratory activity. The *apneustic center* is in the middle and caudal pons and has strong tonic effects on the medullary inspiratory center. Therefore, when there is an upper pontine lesion destroying the pneumotaxic center, the apneustic center's tonic inspiratory influence is in control, and the patient has apneustic breathing (inspiratory cramp). Stretch receptors from the visceral pleura travel via the vagus to the nucleus solitarius and then to the medullary reticular formation to inhibit the medial reticular formation when the lungs are distended (Hering-Breuer reflex). The reverse happens with expiration, with inhibition of the expiratory medullary reticular formation. Phrenic nerves for movement of the diaphragms are from C^3 to C^5.

Vasomotor activity is also centered in the brainstem. The medullary reticular formation has both vasoconstrictor and dilator areas. The roof of the medulla also has sympathetic centers for both constriction and dilation and a parasympathetic center (dorsal efferent nucleus of vagus) primarily for slowing the heart rate. The intensity of the sympathetic activity is in response to the carbon dioxide level in extracellular fluid and results in an increase in arterial pressure. For example, with an intracranial pressure increase there is compression of the vessels at the base, with a resultant local increase of carbon monoxide and a subsequent rise in blood pressure. If the rise in blood pressure fails to overcome the level of intracranial pressure increase, then damage to the vasomotor center occurs, and blood pressure drops to the level of no tonic vasomotor activity (40 to 50 mm Hg). The cortex and hypothalamus also exert some control.

Ascending influences include the baroreceptor system located in the arch of the aorta and the wall of the internal carotid artery. A pressure increase stretches the vessel walls, and impulses travel by nerves IX and X to the nucleus solitarius and then to the reticular substance and dorsal efferent nucleus, so that there is a decrease in sympathetic tone and thus vasodilation, as well as a slowing of heart rate and a decrease in strength of cardiac contraction. If the pressure falls, then the system reverses and there is a loss of inhibitory effect.

Chemoreceptors are located in the aortic glomus and carotid glomus, and they are sensitive to hypoxia. Hypoxia sensed by those peripheral chemoreceptors, is transmitted via nerve IX and X to the nucleus solitarius inducing hyperventilation, whereas hypercapnea (probably really a decreased pH) is sensed by medullary respiratory centers, which induce hyperventilation.

COMMON BRAINSTEM SYNDROMES

A useful grasp of the cross-sectional anatomy of the brainstem is best achieved by understanding some of the classic brainstem syndromes secondary to vascular disease. Any destructive brainstem lesion can be localized in a similar fashion. These are described by occlusion of medial penetrating vessels (short or long), paramedial penetrating vessels, or lateral (circumferential) vessels and in terms of whether this infarction is in the medulla, pons, or midbrain.

Dejerine's syndrome is now called the *medial medullary syndrome*. Its extent is determined by whether short and/or long vessels are occluded. It is also called the anterior spinal artery syndrome. As might be predicted, there is ipsilateral flaccid tongue weakness (from XII nerve loss), contralateral hemiplegia of arm and leg (from pyramidal infarction), and contralateral loss of position and vibration (from infarction of the medial lemniscus) (see Fig. 6A).

The *medial pontine syndrome* from occlusion of medial penetrating pontine vessels (formerly Millard-Gubler syndrome) results in an ipsilateral lateral rectus palsy (exiting VI nerve fibers) and contralateral hemiplegia, including some facial weakness (corticospinal and corticobulbar tracts). If the long medial vessel is involved, then there is extension to the medial lemniscus and medial longitudinal fasciculus; thus there are added losses of vibration and position senses contralaterally and ipsilateral loss of conjugate gaze (internuclear ophthalmoplegia) (see Fig. 6B).

The *medial midbrain syndrome* (formerly Weber's syndrome) produces an ipsilateral complete third cranial nerve palsy (roots of cranial nerve III) and contralateral hemiplegia with face and tongue involvement (from corticospinal and corticobulbar tract infarction) (see Fig. 6C).

There are few well-defined paramedial syndromes, perhaps because of additional vascular supply from medial or lateral vessels. The most often recognized is the *paramedial midbrain syndrome* (formerly Benedikt's syndrome), which results in an ipsilateral third nerve palsy (from root fibers of cranial nerve III), contralateral ataxia and intention tremor of the arm (red nucleus), and sometimes contralateral loss of position and vibration sense (medial lemniscus) and pain and temperature sense (lateral spinothalamic and ventral secondary ascending tract of cranial nerve V) (see Fig. 6D).

The *lateral syndromes* are clearly defined, and the one secondary to infarction of the posterior inferior cerebellar artery (PICA) is the most common of brainstem infarctions. Actually, this occurs more frequently from vertebral artery occlusion, but the infarction seen is in the distribution of Pica. This *lateral medullary syndrome* (Wallenberg's syndrome) has the following manifestations: ipsilateral laryngeal and pharyngeal paralysis (including the vocal cord) caused by infarction of the nucleus ambiguus or roots of nerve X; ipsilateral analgesia and decreased gag response caused by infarction of the nucleus solitarius or nerve IX rootlets; ipsilateral loss of pain and temperature sense from the face caused by infarction of the descending tract and nucleus of nerve V; contralateral loss of pain and temperature sense from the body caused by lateral spinothalamic damage; vertigo, nystagmus, and vomiting caused by vestibular nuclear damage; and ipsilateral cerebellar signs caused by destruction of the inferior cerebellar peduncle. There is also an ipsilateral Horner's syndrome caused by interruption of the descending sympathetic pathway from the hypothalamus that is destined for synapse at spinal cord levels C-8-T-1. The sympathetic tract then synapses in the superior cervical ganglion with postganglionic fibers traveling with the internal carotid artery for distribution to the eye and facial sweat glands. Horner's syndrome or oculosympathetic paralysis produces miosis (small pupil), ptosis (dropped lid), anhidrosis (loss of facial sweating), and enophthalmos (the eye appears minimally retracted in the orbit) (see Fig. 6E).

The *inferior lateral pontine syndrome* (formerly Foville's syndrome) is caused by infarction of the anterior inferior cerebellar artery. This syndrome produces the following manifestations: an ipsilateral lower motor neuron facial weakness (including the forehead) and loss of taste from the anterior two-thirds of the tongue caused by infarction of the nucleus or roots of nerve VII, ipsilateral deafness caused by damage to the roots or nucleus of nerve VIII, ipsilateral loss of pain and temperature sense over the face caused by involvement of the spinal nucleus and descending tract of nerve V, contralateral loss of pain and temperature sense on the body caused by lateral spinothalamic damage, ipsilateral loss of conjugate gaze caused by damage to the pontine center for lateral gaze, and ipsilateral Horner's syndrome caused by damage to the descending sympathetic tract (see Fig. 6F).

The *superior lateral pontine syndrome,* caused by infarction of the superior cerebellar artery, produces ipsilateral intention tremor of the arm and leg caused by infarction of the superior cerebellar peduncle, contralateral loss of pain and temperature sense of face and body caused by destruction of the lateral spinothalamic and ventral ascending tract of nerve V, and ipsilateral Horner's syndrome caused by loss of the descending sympathetic tract.

These syndromes, the structures responsible for their signs and symptoms, and the responsible vessels are outlined in Table 2. Signs and symptoms of posterior cerebral artery infarction are included to complete the pattern of vertebrobasilar occlusive disease (see Fig. 6G).

DISORDERS OF THE OLFACTORY NERVE

Unfortunately, the olfactory nerve is frequently not tested by the clinician unless the patient complains about a loss of the sense of smell or taste. This nerve is best tested by having the patient state not what he smells, but whether he can smell a nonirritative aroma (ie, coffee). Factors that produce a loss of the sense of smell are listed in Table 3. Olfactory hallucinations are frequently associated with temporal lobe seizures (see Chapter 1).

DISORDERS OF THE OPTIC NERVE

Loss of vision must be carefully investigated. One must ascertain whether it was sudden or progressive, unilateral or bilateral, transient or permanent, painful or painless, and associated with other neurologic or ophthalmologic impairment or isolated. Many causes of visual loss are not secondary to involvement of the neural apparatus but result from disease of the cornea, lens, media, or retina. This can be appreciated by ophthalmoscopic examination. The patient must have a best corrected visual acuity, plotted visual fields, and ophthalmodynamometry, in addition to a thorough ocular and neurologic physical examination. Further studies may then be indicated.

The term *amblyopia* means a visual defect without any recognizable lesion of the eye, thought to be secondary to defective retinal sensation. Neurologic (nerve or brain) visual loss is called *amaurosis,* although this term is frequently used in a broader sense to designate blindness of any etiology. *Primary optic atrophy* refers to an opaque white disk, with very sharp margins, decreased disk capillaries, narrowed retinal vessels, and often an increased physiologic cup with visible lamina cribrosa. Primary atrophy designates some insult to the optic nerve itself that has resulted in nerve degeneration. *Secondary optic atrophy* may look less chalky white, with the margins not as starkly distinct because of glial tissue, and the lamina cribrosa not visible. It results from processes causing morphologic visible change in the optic nerve head prior to progression of atrophy. Therefore any cause of papilledema can result in secondary optic atrophy, and many authorities class the destruction by optic neuritis as also leading to secondary rather than primary optic atrophy. In primary and secondary atrophy, acuity is diminished, and the visual fields become concentrically contracted. The fields of secondary atrophy may also reveal the defect of disk elevation or the primary intracranial problem. An extensive review of neuroophthalmologic problems cannot be undertaken in this overview; therefore only the more common causes of visual loss, field defects, and pupillary abnormalities will be covered.

Table 4 lists the diseases that may produce unilateral visual loss. Table 5 lists the causes of optic atrophy. The differential diagnosis among papilledema, optic neuritis, and retrobulbar neuritis can be found in Table 6.

Blurring of the disk, however, does not have to be pathologic; it can be seen with the following: (1) hyaline bodies of disk (Drusen), (2) pseudopapilledema, (3) hyperoptic astigmatism, and (4) congenital persistence of myelin sheath or retinal fibers.

Table 7 lists the etiologies underlying common visual field defects.

DIPLOPIA

Diplopia results from a dissociation of conjugate gaze. It is important for the history to note the rapidity of onset, whether it is periodic or progressive, whether it varies with fatigue, whether it disappears when one eye is covered, and whether it is greater in the horizontal or vertical plane. Other ocular abnormalities may lead to localization (eg, pupillary defects, ptosis, or nystagmus). Diplopia can be monocular, with ectopia lentis, corneal irregularities, or early cataract. Additionally physiologic diplopia (ie, the difference between the two eyes that is integrated by higher cortical centers to allow depth and dimension to objects) may be accentuated by depressants (eg, alcohol).

Pathologic diplopia occurs when an object being viewed is not projected on the macula of each eye. The separation of images will be greater as the patient gazes in the direction of the paretic muscle because the image falling on the macula of the normal eye is being projected farther from the macula onto the retina of the abnormal eye. This also explains why the peripheral image always defines the involved eye. Finally, the image from the abnormal eye is the fake image and will be less clear because it is not being viewed by the most sensitive visual apparatus, the macula.

Generally speaking, a double image is caused by a loss of conjugate gaze and could occur with disease of the extraocular cranial nerve nuclei, connections correlating the actions of yoked muscles, eg, vestibular and especially medial longitudinal fasciculus, nerves III, IV, or VI, the extraocular muscles themselves, or processes that physically limit globe movement. The differential diagnosis of diplopia is listed in Table 8.

PUPILLARY ABNORMALITIES

The pupil is a useful guide to localization. If anisocoria is present, the examiner must decide which pupil is abnormal and then search for associated abnormalities (eg, ptosis and anhidrosis of Horner's syndrome). The responses to direct and consensual light and to accommodation are critical, because a dilated fixed pupil means an efferent problem (III nerve to sphincter) a pupil reacting less well to light indicates an optic nerve lesion (this may require the swinging flashlight test) (see Tables 4, 5, 6, and 7), a pupil reacting better to accommodation effort than to light indicates an Argyll Robertson pupil of syphillis, a pupil sluggish to light and accommodation that is dilated in ordinary room light and that constricts with prolonged stimulation is an Adie's tonic pupil perhaps secondary to ciliary ganglion disease. In addition to examination of the direct, consensual, and accommodative pupillary reflexes, certain pharmacologic tests have been useful in diagnosing and localizing pupillary abnormalities.

Pharmacologic Tests for Horner's Syndrome and Adie's Syndrome

Autonomic Neuroanatomy. (see Fig. 7.) Parasympathetic impulses originate in the nucleus of Edinger-Westphal and travel on the outside rim of cranial nerve III. Synapses occur in the ciliary ganglion and fibers then travel to ciliary muscle and to the sphincter of the pupil. These postganglionic fibers are cholinergic, with approximately 97 percent of fibers in the ciliary ganglion subserving the ciliary muscle for accommodation.

First-order neurons carrying sympathetic impulses arise in the posterolateral hypothalamus and descend through the midbrain in the region of the red nucleus and through the brainstem in the lateral tract group; they synapse on neurons of intermediate lateral gray matter at the C-8-T-2 level. Preganglionic fibers then travel up the sympathetic chain to the superior cervical ganglion and synapse. The postganglionic fibers then ascend on the carotid artery, reaching the eye along the ophthalmic artery, to terminate as adrenergic endings on the pupilodilator fibers of the iris. Similar postganglionic fibers end on levator muscles of the lid and sweat glands of the face.

Horner's Syndrome. Interruption of any of the three sympathetic neuron pathways should give rise to Horner's syndrome. Adrenergic endings tonically release small amounts of transmitter, which are then resorbed by the nerve endings. This reuptake may be blocked by drugs, allowing transmitter to accumulate. Destruction of any nerve ending will promote the phenomenon of denervation hypersensitivity to the transmitter substance in the effector organ.

Cocaine Test. Cocaine blocks reuptake of released adrenergic transmitter by the postganglionic fibers; it is also an MAO inhibitor. Consequently, when two drops of a 4 percent solution of cocaine are instilled in a normal eye, norepinephrine accumulates, dilating the pupil. In a Horner's eye, the nerve endings either are absent or are hypoactive, and cocaine has little effect, if any. Theoretically, a postganglionic lesion should have no nerve endings, and therefore there should be no effect of cocaine. Preganglionic or central lesions, on the other hand, have postganglionic fibers intact, but they are hypoactive; hence cocaine will have some effect but not to the same degree as in a normal eye. However, difficulties arise when lesions are incomplete. The test is performed by instilling two drops of 4 percent cocaine in each eye. An effect should be seen within 15 to 20 minutes, with the normal eye serving as a control. Theoretically, a postganglionic lesion will show no response, a central lesion will show some dilatation (but not to the same degree as in the normal eye), and a preganglionic lesion will have an intermediate response.

Epinephrine Test. The epinephrine test utilizes the phenomenon of denervation hypersensitivity. A dilute solution (1:1000) of epinephrine is instilled into each eye *after* the cocaine test. This should have no effect in the normal eye, but in the Horner's eye denervation hypersensitivity should allow the pupil to dilate. Theoretically, a postganglionic lesion should have complete denervation (and consequently more marked dilatation), and a central lesion should have less denervation. Again, this distinction is complicated by the presence of incomplete lesions.

Tonic Pupil or Adie's Syndrome. The Adie's pupil is dilated and reacts sluggishly to light, if it reacts at all. It contracts sluggishly to near accommodation and sluggishly returns to its dilated state at the return to far fixation. It is usually unilateral but may be bilateral, and it is often associated with lower extremity hyporeflexia. It is thought to result from damage to the ciliary ganglion and subsequent abnormal reinnervation. Since about 97 percent of the fibers of the ciliary ganglion subserve the ciliary muscle and only 3 percent subserve the pupillary sphincter, after damage to the ganglion the ciliary muscle nerves are most likely to regenerate. Consequently, the pupillary sphincter muscle is now innervated by accommodative fibers. In addition, the pupillary sphincter muscle will exhibit denervation hypersensitivity to its transmitter, acetylcholine.

Methacholine (Mecholyl) is a parasympathomimetic drug, simulating acetylcholine. When a dilute solution of methacholine (2.5 percent) is instilled into each eye, the normal eye will not react, but the tonic pupil will constrict.

DISORDERS OF THE TRIGEMINAL NERVE

Cranial nerve V has motor and sensory functions. The sensory roots are separate and travel through individual foramina, thus isolating pain or numbness to mandibular (V^3), maxillary (V^2), or ophthalmic (V^1) divisions. The motor division runs with the mandibular portion, and weakness of mastication is therefore more likely to be associated with V^3 sensory abnormalities. Table 9 lists some of the diseases that may affect V nerve function.

DISORDERS OF THE FACIAL NERVE

Cranial nerve VII is frequently damaged as an isolated event (Bell's palsy), or it may be involved in more widespread pathology. There are two components to this nerve: a motor division and the intermediate nerve of Wrisberg, which conveys parasympathetic and sensory fibers. The parasympathetic fibers innervate the submandibular and sublingual glands through the submandibular ganglion, as well as the nasal mucosa and lacrimal glands through the pterygopalatine ganglion. Sensory fibers from the posterior external auditory meatus, mastoid area, and nasopharyngeal mucosa and taste fibers from the anterior two-thirds of the tongue are also relayed. The site of involvement of cranial nerve VII can be well localized, as outlined in Table 10. Table 11 lists some of the diseases causing dysfunction of cranial nerve VII.

DISORDERS OF THE ACOUSTIC AND VESTIBULAR SYSTEM: DEAFNESS, DIZZINESS, AND NYSTAGMUS

Disorders of the cochlea, labyrinth, and nerve VIII or its central connections may produce deafness (Tables 12 and 13) and dizziness (Tables 14 and 15). Nystagmus is a rhythmic involuntary movement of the eyes. Most nystagmus has a slow phase and a fast phase, with the direction of nystagmus conventionally named for the fast phase. The slow phase has characteristics of a pursuit eye movement, with the fast phase being saccadic. Pendular nystagmus has no fast and slow phases and is therefore an exception. Nystagmus can be physiologic or hysterical, or it may be secondary to ocular, vestibular, brainstem and cerebellar pathways, or cerebral dysfunction. Nystagmus is usually horizontal, but it can be vertical up, vertical down, oblique, rotatory, or retractory. The eyes usually move conjugately, but they may be dissociated. First-degree nystagmus is that present when looking in the direction of the fast phase only; second-degree nystagmus is nystagmus present on forward gaze; and third-degree nystagmus is persistence of the fast phase in one direction even when looking in the opposite direction. Third-degree nystagmus is usually transient and is due to peripheral disease, while first-degree nystagmus is more permanent and is of central etiology. Monocular nystagmus is a curiosity that is poorly understood. The types of nystagmus are listed in Table 16.

DISORDERS OF THE GLOSSOPHARYNGEAL (IX), VAGUS (X), ACCESSORY (XI), AND HYPOGLOSSAL (XII) NERVES

The lower four cranial nerves have their nuclei in the medulla and are closely approximated until leaving the skull. For these reasons the pathologic processes involving these nerves are similar; they will be outlined as a unit in Table 17.

TABLE 1

Cranial Nerves

Motor plate: (1) Somatic motor function is served by cranial nerves III, IV, VI, and XII, which are all in the midline of the brainstem and simply represent an interrupted homologue of the spinal cord ventral horn. (2) Branchial motor nuclei are the nuclei giving rise to derivatives of the branchial arch mesoderm; they are divided into (a) visceral motor (also called general visceral efferent), which are simply the nuclei giving rise to the cranial preganglionic parasympathetics (III, Edinger-Westphal; VII, nervus intermedius; IX, lesser superficial petrosal nerve; X, vagus), and (b) muscle function (also called special visceral efferent) (V, motor root; VII, motor root; X, vagus; XI, accessory).

Sensory plate: (1) The visceral sensory zone that is the medial part of the sensory plate is called the nucleus solitarius. This receives information from VII, IX, and X and takes care of all general visceral afferent information coming from everywhere about the head except for the classic distribution of cranial nerve V and part of the ear, mastoid, external auditory meatus, and tympanic membrane. It also receives special visceral afferent information (taste). (2) The general somatic zone is V, including mesencephalic, chief sensory, and descending nuclei. Pain and temperature input from the ear, etc, carried by IX and X, still goes to the descending nucleus of V. (3) Special somatic nuclei are cochlear and vestibular nuclei.

NERVE	NUCLEUS AND LOCATION	FORAMEN AND/OR SPECIAL NERVES	GANGLION	FUNCTION
Olfactory		Cribriform plate		Smell
Optic II	Lateral geniculate; thalamus	Optic canal		Vision
Oculomotor III	Motor; midbrain	Superior orbital fissure		Medial rectus, adduction; superior rectus, pure elevator with eye abducted 23° (up and out function), pure intorter with eye adducted 67°; inferior rectus, pure depressor with eye abducted 23° (down and out function), pure extorter with eye adducted 67°; inferior oblique, pure elevator with eye adducted 51° (up and in function), pure extorter with eye abducted 39°

	Edinger-Westphal; midbrain	Superior orbital fissure	Ciliary	Pupillary constriction
Trochlear IV	Midbrain	Superior orbital fissure		Superior oblique, pure depressor with eye adducted 51° (down and in function), pure intorter with eye abducted 39°
Trigeminal V	Motor; pons	Ovale traveling with mandibular		Mouth closure: masseter, temporalis, pterygoids; jaw protrusion: pterygoids; side-to-side movement: pterygoids; opening: digastric, mylohyoid, with external pterygoid pulling mandible forward; also to tensor tympani and tensor veli palatini
	Mesencephalic; pons and midbrain	Ovale with V^3	Gasserian	Proprioception, face and jaw muscles
	Chief sensory; pons		Gasserian	Touch
	Descending; pons → C^3		Gasserian	Pain and temperature
	V^1; ophthalmic	Superior orbital fissure		
	V^2; maxillary	Rotundum		
	V^3; mandibular	Ovale		
Abducens VI	Pons	Superior orbital fissure		Lateral rectus for abduction
Facial VII	Motor; pons	Internal auditory meatus with branch to stapedius		Muscles of facial expression except levator palpebrae; to buccinator, platysma, stylohyoid, posterior belly digastric
	Superior salivatory	Nervus intermedius → chorda tympani → lingual	Submaxillary	Parasympathetic to submaxillary and sublingual glands
	Solitarius (pons)	Lingual → chorda tympani (nervus intermedius)	Geniculate	Taste, anterior two-thirds of tongue
	Lacrimal (superior salivatory)	Greater superficial petrosal and vidian	Sphenopalatine	Lacrimal and nasal glands

TABLE 1 (CONT.)

NERVE	NUCLEUS AND LOCATION	FORAMEN AND/OR SPECIAL NERVES	GANGLION	FUNCTION
Vestibular VIII	Superior; Bechterew's nucleus Lateral; Deiters' nucleus Medial; Schwalbe's nucleus Inferior; Roller's nucleus, pons and medulla	Internal auditory meatus	Scarpa's	Cristae are in ampullas of semicircular canals for rotation; maculas are in utricle and saccule for linear displacement and gravity
Auditory VIII	Ventral and dorsal cochlear in medulla	Internal auditory meatus	Spiral	Hearing
Glossopharyngeal IX	Solitarius; medulla	Jugular foramen	Petrosal	Pain, from area of tympanic membrane, external meatus, ear, and mastoid
	Descending V	Jugular foramen	Petrosal	Taste, from posterior one-third of tongue Pain and temperature, from posterior one-third of tongue, epiglottis, pharynx, posterior soft palate
	Chief sensory of V	Jugular foramen	Petrosal	Tactile, from areas above
	Ambiguus; medulla	Jugular foramen	Petrosal	Stylopharyngeus muscle that is an elevator of upper pharynx; muscles of anterior and posterior pillars of fauces for swallowing;
	Inferior salivatory medulla	Tympanic branch (Jacobsen's), lesser superficial petrosal	Otic, with postganglionic via auriculotemporal nerve	salivary secretion from parotid gland

Nerve	Nucleus	Exit	Ganglion	Function
Vagus X	Solitarius; medulla	Jugular foramen	Nodose	Pain, from lower pharynx, larynx, bronchi, trachea, esophagus, stomach, most of GI tract, heart; taste from epiglottis
	Descending V	Jugular foramen	Nodose (Arnold nerve)	Pain, from tympanic membrane, external meatus, ear, mastoid
	Chief sensory of V	Jugular foramen	Nodose	Tactile, from the pharynx, etc, above where pain goes to solitarius
	Ambiguus; medulla			Laryngeal muscles (cricothyroid, abductors, adductors), muscles of soft palate, except tensor veli palatini; muscles of pharynx, except stylopharyngeus
Accessory XI	Ambiguus and C^{1-4}	Fibers C^{1-4} ascend through foramen magnum and join cranial part and exit through jugular foramen		Sternocleidomastoid has bilateral supranuclear innervation with ipsilateral predominance. Function is to turn head in opposite direction; upper one-half trapezius is ambigus and C^{3-4}. With weakness upper part of scapula is displaced down with vertebral border flared; lower trapezius has only cervical innervation.
Hypoglossal XII	Hypoglossal	Hypoglossal canal with branch to ansa hypoglossi		Supplies the intrinsic tongue muscles and hypoglossus, styloglossus, and genioglossus (most important for tongue protrusion); most of these muscles have bilateral innervation, but genioglossus may have mostly contralateral innervation; a cortical lesion rarely gives tongue deviation, but subcortical may, with tongue deviating to side of lesion because of unopposed opposite genioglossus

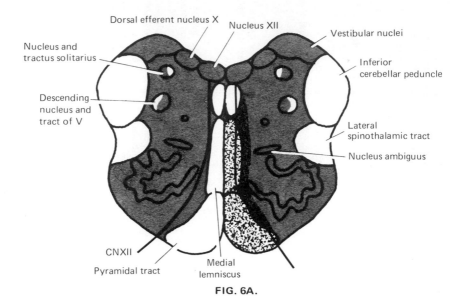

Dorsal efferent nucleus X   Nucleus XII

Vestibular nuclei

Nucleus and tractus solitarius

Inferior cerebellar peduncle

Descending nucleus and tract of V

Lateral spinothalamic tract

Nucleus ambiguus

CNXII

Pyramidal tract

Medial lemniscus

FIG. 6A.

Medial longitudinal fasciculus

Ventricle IV

Descending nucleus and tract V

Pontine paramedian reticular formation

Lateral spinothalamic tract

Nucleus VI

Motor nucleus CNVII

Superior olive

Medial lemniscus

CNVII

CNVI

Corticospinal and corticobulbar fibers

FIG. 6B.

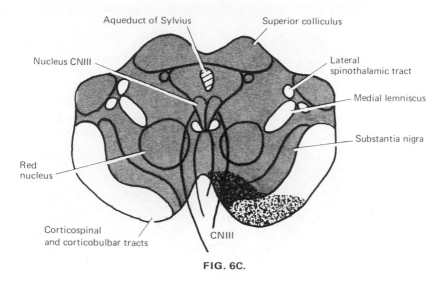

Aqueduct of Sylvius

Superior colliculus

Nucleus CNIII

Lateral spinothalamic tract

Medial lemniscus

Substantia nigra

Red nucleus

Corticospinal and corticobulbar tracts

CNIII

FIG. 6C.

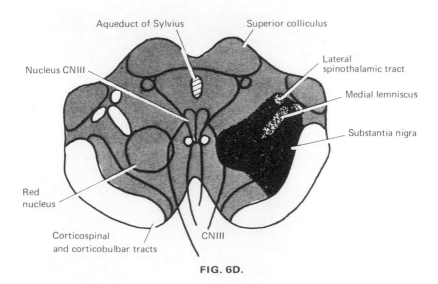

Aqueduct of Sylvius

Superior colliculus

Nucleus CNIII

Lateral spinothalamic tract

Medial lemniscus

Substantia nigra

Red nucleus

Corticospinal and corticobulbar tracts

CNIII

FIG. 6D.

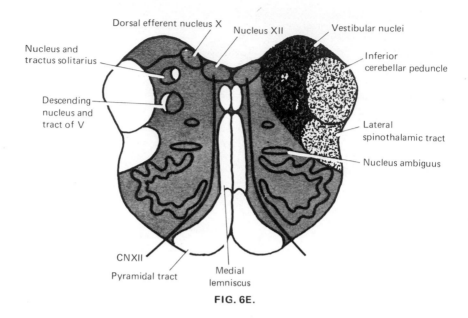

FIG. 6E.

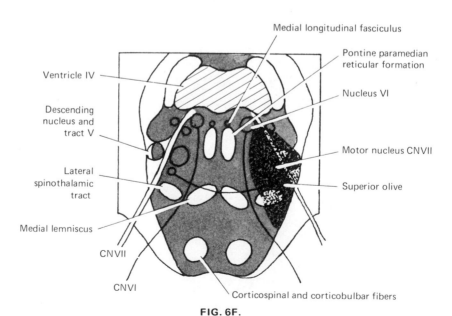

FIG. 6F.

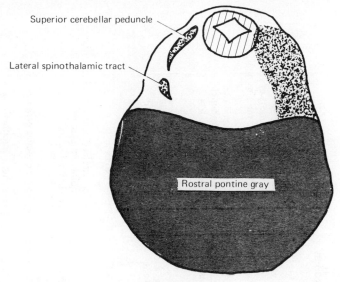

Superior cerebellar peduncle

Lateral spinothalamic tract

Rostral pontine gray

FIG. 6G.

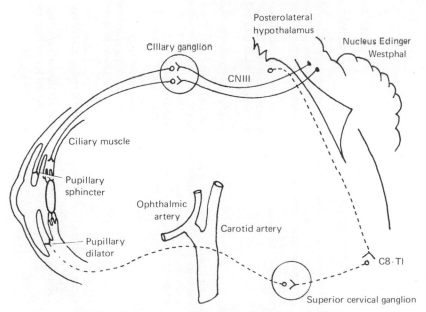

Posterolateral
hypothalamus

Ciliary ganglion

Nucleus Edinger
Westphal

CNIII

Ciliary muscle

Pupillary
sphincter

Ophthalmic
artery

Carotid artery

Pupillary
dilator

C8-TI

Superior cervical ganglion

FIG. 7. Autonomic neuroanatomy of pupillary control.

TABLE 2

Classic Brainstem Syndromes

SYNDROME	FINDINGS	STRUCTURE
Lateral medullary syndrome; also known as Wallenberg's syndrome, posterior inferior cerebellar artery (PICA) syndrome, lateral medullary plate	Voice change from ipsilateral vocal cord paralysis	Nucleus ambiguus or roots of X
	Ipsilateral decreased gag response	Nucleus solitarius or roots of IX
	Ipsilateral loss of pain and temperature sensation on face	Descending tract and nucleus of V
	Ipsilateral Horner's syndrome	Descending sympathetic tract
	Ipsilateral cerebellar findings	Inferior cerebellar peduncle
	Contralateral loss of pain and temperature sensation of body	Lateral spinothalamic tract
	Vertigo, nystagmus, vomiting	Vestibular nuclei
Inferior lateral pontine syndrome; also known as Foville's syndrome, anterior inferior cerebellar artery syndrome	Ipsilateral lower motor neuron facial weakness and loss of taste sensation on anterior-two-thrids of tongue	VII
	Ipsilateral deafness	VIII
	Ipsilateral loss of pain and temperature sensation on face	Descending V
	Ipsilateral loss of horizontal conjugate gaze	Pontine paramedial reticular formation
	Ipsilateral Horner's syndrome	Descending sympathetic
	Contralateral loss of pain and temperature sensation of body	Lateral spinothalamic
Superior lateral pontine syndrome; also known as superior cerebellar artery syndrome	Ipsilateral ataxia and intention tremor of arm and leg	Superior cerebellar peduncle
	Ipsilateral Horner's syndrome	Descending sympathetic
	Contralateral loss of pain and temperature sensation on face and body	Lateral spinothalamic and ventral ascending V

Syndrome	Clinical findings	Structure involved
Posterior cerebral artery syndrome	Loss of sensation on contralateral body with concomitant pain	Thalamus
	Hemiballismus	Subthalamus
	Field defect	Occipital lobe
	Material specific memory defect	Unilateral medial temporal lobe
	Global amnesia	Bilateral medial temporal lobe or ischemia of one temporal lobe with the other previously damaged
Medial medullary syndrome; also known as Dejerine's syndrome, anterior spinal artery syndrome, alternating inferior hemiplegia	Ipsilateral flaccid tongue weakness	XII
	Contralateral hemiplegia	Pyramidal tract
	Sometimes contralateral loss of position and vibration sensation	Medial lemniscus
Medial pontine syndrome; also known as Millard-Gubler syndrome, medial penetrating pontine arteries, alternating middle hemiplegia	Ipsilateral lateral rectus palsy	VI nerve
	Contralateral hemiplegia with face usually involved	Corticospinal and corticobulbar tracts
	Sometimes contralateral loss position and vibration sensation	Medial lemniscus
	Sometimes loss of adduction of ipsilateral eye during conjugate gaze	MLF
Medial midbrain syndrome; also known as Weber's syndrome, medial penetrating midbrain artery, superior alternating hemiplegia	Ipsilateral complete III nerve palsy	III rootlets
	Contralateral hemiplegia	Corticospinal and corticobulbar tracts
Paramedial midbrain syndrome	Ipsilateral complete third nerve palsy, so that the eye is down and out, the lid has ptosis, and the pupil is dilated and not responsive to light	Roots of III
	Contralateral ataxia and intention tremor of arm	Red nucleus and decussation of superior cerebellar peduncle after its crossover
	Sometimes contralateral loss of position and vibration sensation	Medial lemniscus
	Sometimes contralateral loss of pain and temperature sensation	Lateral spinothalamic tract and ventral secondary ascending tract of V

TABLE 3

Factors That May Produce Defects in Olfaction

DEGENERATIVE
  Senility

TOXIC
  Smoking
  Amphetamines
  Cocaine
  Lead
  Cadmium

METABOLIC
  Pernicious anemia

VASCULAR
  Arteriosclerosis
  Anterior cerebral artery aneurysm

INFECTIOUS
  Meningitis
  Frontal abscess
  Osteomyelitis of cribriform plate
  Sinusitis
  Herpes

TRAUMATIC
  Fracture of ethmoids, cribriform plate
  Tearing of olfactory filaments by shearing effect

NEOPLASTIC
  Sphenoid ridge or olfactory groove (meningiomas)
  Frontal lobe (gliomas)
  Parasellar lesions

OTHER
  Hysteria

TABLE 4

Unilateral Visual Loss

Neurologic causes of unilateral visual deficit are usually associated with decreased pupillary response to light. This may be obvious on direct testing or may be seen as only a relative deficit when compared with the consensual response in the abnormal eye to light presented to the normal eye (swinging flashlight test or Marcus Gunn phenomenon).

COMMON NONNEUROLOGIC ETIOLOGIES
Inflammatory processes
Glaucoma
Cataract
Macular degeneration

COMMON NEUROLOGIC ETIOLOGIES
Optic neuritis
Retrobulbar neuritis
Ischemia
Intracranial aneurysm
Optic nerve neoplasms
Prechiasmal neoplasms
Some chiasmal neoplasms with nerve involvement
Trauma
Other causes of optic atrophy (See Table 5)

TABLE 5

Optic Atrophy

PRIMARY OPTIC ATROPHY

Degenerative
    Multiple sclerosis
    Nutritional (vitamin deficiency or starvation, perhaps alcohol amblyopia)
    Paget's disease of bone
    Hand-Schüller-Christian disease
    Tay-Sachs disease
    Niemann-Pick disease
    Laurence-Moon-Biedl syndrome
    Fibrous dysplasia

Toxic
    Tobacco–alcohol amblyopia
    Lead
    Methyl alcohol
    Aniline
    Tri-*o*-cresyl phosphate
    Tryparsamide (pentavalent arsenical)
    Salicylates
    Carbon disulfide
    Thallium

Metabolic
    Addison's disease
    Diabetes (vascular)
    Uremia
    Pernicious anemia
    Hyperthyroidism
    Toxemia

Vascular
    Ischemia of optic nerve (arteriosclerosis)
    Anemia
    Aneurysmal compression
    Arteritis (especially temporal arteritis)
    Spasm

Infectious
    Viral (eg, influenza)
    Parasitic
    Fungal
    Post inoculation
    Lues (especially tabes dorsalis)
    Polyneuritis
    Meningitis (bacterial, tuberculous)

Trauma
    Optic nerve trauma

TABLE 5 (CONT'D.)

Neoplasm
  Orbital
  Optic nerve glioma
  Pituitary
  Craniopharyngioma
  Metastatic
  Meningiomas of sphenoid wing, olfactory groove
  Frontal lobe
  Retinoblastoma or melanoma extending into nerve
  Osteosarcoma

Congenital/Hereditary
  Leber's hereditary optic atrophy
  Oxycephaly

SECONDARY OPTIC ATROPHY

Papillitis
  Virtually the same differential as primary optic atrophy; the process occurs near the
  disk, and the disk is therefore swollen during the acute phase, with visual loss; the resultant atrophy shows the gray white color of gliosis

Papilledema
  Swelling of the optic disk from increased intracranial pressure (see Chapter 8)
  without impairment of vision

TABLE 6

Differentiation of Papilledema, Optic Neuritis, Retrobulbar Neuritis

SIGNS AND SYMPTOMS	PAPILLEDEMA	OPTIC NEURITIS	RETROBULBAR NEURITIS
Ocular pain	0	+	+
Photophobia	0	+	+
Visual complaint	0 (unless very late with optic atrophy)	+	+
Laterality	Usually both eyes	One eye usually, although may be consecutive	One eye usually, although may be consecutive
Pupil response to light	Normal	Decreased to direct light; may require swinging flashlight test	Decreased to direct light; may require swinging flashlight test
Acuity	Normal	Decreased	Decreased
Fields	Enlarged blind spot	Central or cecocentral scotoma ± enlarged blind spot	Central or cecocentral scotoma
Disk swelling	4+ (late)	2+	0
Hemorrhages	4+ (late)	1+	0

TABLE 7

Common Visual Field Defects

RETINAL LESIONS

Retinitis pigmentosa: ring scotomas greater for blue than red

Chorioretinitis: defect corresponding to destroyed retina

Vascular: arteriosclerosis, embolism, spasm, arteritis can occlude the central retinal artery and produce a blind eye or occlude only a branch and produce a sharp sector defect

OPTIC DISK LESIONS

Glaucoma: the defective fields result from a circulatory disturbance to nerve fibers on or near the disk; early evidence is extension (usually upward) of the blind spot, Seidel scotoma, or an isolated ill-defined scotoma; the scotoma then enlarges in an arcuate fashion over the fixation point and extends to the horizontal raphe (Bjerrum scotoma); with nasal contraction the scotoma becomes peripheral, and the horizontal step nasally between normal and absent vision is called the nasal step of Ronne; ring scotomas can occur.

Papilledema: enlarged blind spot and later contraction of the fields if secondary optic atrophy is present

OPTIC NERVE LESIONS

The fields show scotomas (especially central or cecocentral), contractions or blindness of one or both eyes (one eye only is definitely prechiasmal); the common etiologies are listed below, and a more complete differential diagnosis can be found in Table 5 on optic atrophy

Tumors: meningioma (sphenoid ridge or olfactory groove); pituitary adenoma that extends rostrally or pushes the optic nerve against a superior, more fixed structure (eg, the anterior cerebral artery)

Aneurysm: carotid, anterior cerebral

Trauma

Infections: luetic interstitial optic neuritis with arachnoiditis, tuberculous or bacterial meningitic arachnoiditis

Demyelinating: multiple sclerosis, Devic's disease

TABLE 7 (CONT.)

CHIASMAL LESIONS

The characteristic field defect is bitemporal hemianopsia; variations depend on whether there is added optic nerve encroachment (anterior chiasmal) or optic tract involvement (posterior chiasmal)

Tumors: chromophobe adenoma, eosinophilic adenoma, craniopharyngioma, meningioma of tuberculum sellae, astrocytoma, chordoma, metastatic

Vascular: aneurysms of internal carotid, anterior cerebral, or anterior communicating artery

Arachnoiditis

Trauma: usually fatal

Third ventricle dilatation

Demyelinating: multiple sclerosis

POSTCHIASMAL LESIONS

Posterior lesions are more congruous because the fibers representing congruous portions of the visual field are very close; similarly, optic tract lesions are very incongruous because the fibers are separated; macular sparing may be present in occipital lesions because of overlapping blood supply from middle cerebral and posterior cerebral arteries to the occipital pole; lesions will not cause a field defect that crosses the vertical meridian. Occipital lobe causes a congruous homonymous defect with macular sparing. Temporal lobe causes less congruous upper quadrant defects extending to the point of fixation (without macular sparing); the lower fibers that course anteriorly around the inferior horn of the lateral ventricle (Meyer's loop) give rise to peripheral upper quadrant defects (pie-in-the-sky defects). Parietal lobe causes less congruous lower quadrant defects with extension to the fixation point. Optic tract causes distinctly incongruous field defects. For etiologies, see Chapter 2, Table 3.

TABLE 8

Etiology of Diplopia

ORBIT
Neoplasm
Traumatic muscle entrapment
Abscess
Hemorrhage
Idiopathic orbital inflammation

MUSCLE
Thyroid eye disease
Surgical malalignment

NEUROMUSCULAR JUNCTION
Myasthenia gravis
Botulism

NERVE
Neoplasms: false localizing sign of increased intracranial pressure, acoustic neuroma, meningioma, lymphoma, reticulum cell sarcoma, chordoma, pituitary tumor, nasopharyngeal carcinoma, meningeal carcinomatosis, herniation from supratentorial mass

Trauma

Vascular
  Diabetes (pupil sparing III nerve palsy)
  Posterior communicating aneurysm
  Cavernous sinus aneurysm
  Cavernous sinus thrombosis

Infections
  Bacterial
  Luetic
  Tuberculosis
  Miller-Fisher variant of Guillain-Barré syndrome
  Fungal involvement of meninges
  Gradenigo's syndrome
  Granulomatous painful ophthalmoplegia of Tolosa and Hunt

Other
  Sarcoidosis
  Pituitary apoplexy

NUCLEUS AND INTRAMEDULLARY PORTION OF NERVE
Neoplasms: pontine glioma, medulloblastoma, metastatic
Trauma: more often nerve damage
Vascular: arteriosclerotic thrombosis, hemorrhage, arteritis of collagen vascular or infectious nature
Infections: encephalitis, poliomyelitis, postvaccinal encephalomyelitis, fungal
Demyelinating: multiple sclerosis

TABLE 9

Dysfunction of Cranial Nerve V

DYSFUNCTION	CENTRAL	GANGLION	ROOT OR NERVE	PAIN	NUMBNESS	WEAKNESS
Degenerative						
Multiple sclerosis	+ (root entry)			++	+	
Syringobulbia or syringomyelia of upper cervical segments	+				++	
Idiopathic trigeminal neuralgia (?)		+	+	++ (especially V^2, V^3, and less V^1)		
Scleroderma			+	+	+	
Sjögren's syndrome			+		+	
Sarcoidosis			+		+	+
Toxic						
Stilbamidine			+	+	+	
Trichloroethylene			+		+	+
*Vascular**						
Arteritis, lupus		+		+	+	
Cavernous sinus aneurysm or thrombosis			Ophthalmic		+	
Aberrant vascular branches or aneurysms			Root	++	+	

Neoplastic					
Neurinoma	+		+ (late)	+‡	+
Primary or metastatic to face, tongue, sinuses	+	Especially mandibular	+	+	+
Nasopharyngeal	+	+	+	+	+ (late)
Skull-base chondroma, chordoma, sarcoma, meningioma	+	+ (root)	+	+	
Cholesteatoma		+ (root)	++	+	
Traumatic					
Craniofacial		+	+	+‡	+
Basal fractures		Mandibular	+	+	
Dental extractions		+	+		
Infectious					
Herpes zoster	+		++ (especially V¹ by 4:1 ratio)	+	
Postmaxillary sinusitis	+	+	+		
Gradenigo's syndrome (petrous apex)	+		+ (V¹)	+	
Syphillis					
Idiopathic	+	or +	+	+‡	+

*See infarctions (ie, atherosclerotic and embolic) in Table 2.

TABLE 10

Site of Cranial Nerve VII Disruption

SITE	FACIAL WEAKNESS	STAPEDIAL DYSFUNCTION	LACRIMATION	TASTE	ASSOCIATED ABNORMALITIES
Supranuclear	Contralateral lower two-thirds; no Bell's phenomenon; mimetic function better	No	Normal	Normal	Cortical, subcortical, midbrain, or upper pontine structures
Nuclear	Ipsilateral face	Yes	Normal	Normal	Usually part of anterior inferior cerebellar artery syndrome
Genu	Ipsilateral face	Yes	Normal	Normal	Often has associated ipsilateral lateral rectus weakness, horizontal conjugate gaze paresis to same side, or the one-and-one-half syndrome
Posterior fossa and internal auditory meatus pregeniculate ganglion	Ipsilateral face	Yes	↓	↓	Perhaps VIII nerve, V nerve, cerebellar dysfunction; late increased intracranial pressure
Geniculate ganglion	Ipsilateral face	Yes	↓	↓	No deafness or other cranial nerves involved (except rare cases of herpes zoster)
Postgeniculate ganglion to stapedius	Ipsilateral face	Yes	Normal	↓	Same as geniculate
Distal to stapedius to chorda tympani	Ipsilateral face	Normal	Normal	↓	Facial weakness

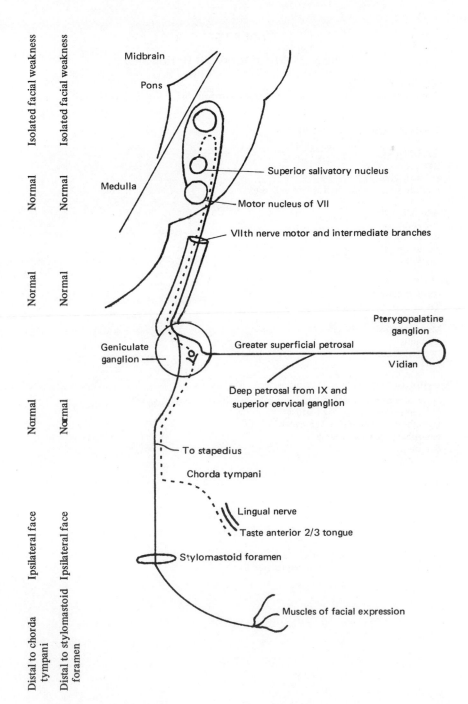

Isolated facial weakness

Isolated facial weakness

Normal

Normal

Normal

Normal

Normal

Normal

Distal to chorda tympani

Ipsilateral face

Distal to stylomastoid foramen

Ipsilateral face

Midbrain

Pons

Superior salivatory nucleus

Medulla

Motor nucleus of VII

VIIth nerve motor and intermediate branches

Geniculate ganglion

Greater superficial petrosal

Pterygopalatine ganglion

Vidian

Deep petrosal from IX and superior cervical ganglion

To stapedius

Chorda tympani

Lingual nerve

Taste anterior 2/3 tongue

Stylomastoid foramen

Muscles of facial expression

TABLE 11

Etiology of Cranial Nerve VII Dysfunction

DEGENERATIVE
Some muscular dystrophies (eg, myotonic dystrophy*)

TOXIC/METABOLIC
Thiamine deficiency*

TRAUMATIC
Basal fracture
Parotid surgery
Birth trauma, especially forceps delivery

VASCULAR
Thrombosis
Embolism
Hemorrhage
Arteritis

INFECTIOUS
Guillain-Barré*
Tuberculous meningitis*
Fungal meningitis*
Mononucleosis*
Syphillis
Herpes zoster
Leprosy

NEOPLASTIC
Cerebellopontine angle (CPA) tumors (neurofibroma, meningioma)
Diffuse meningeal carcinomatosis*
Lymphomas–leukemia (meningeal)*
Nasopharyngeal carcinoma*
Sarcoma*
Parotid tumors

OTHER
Idiopathic (Bell's) palsy
Sarcoidosis*
Parotid sarcoid
Polymyositis*
Myasthenia gravis*
Melkerson's syndrome (painless facial swelling,
    sometimes lingua plicata, often familial)*

Often bilateral.

TABLE 12

Causes of Deafness

CONGENITAL
Maternal rubella
Anoxia
Hyperbilirubinemia
Refsum's disease (phytanic acid)

TOXIC/METABOLIC
Medications
    Antibiotics
    Salicylates
    Quinine
Thiamine deficiency (beriberi)
Pellagra (niacin deficiency)
Hypothyroidism (childhood, cochlear; adult, retrocochlear)
Diabetes

VASCULAR
Occlusion of internal auditory artery
Periarteritis nodosa

TRAUMATIC
Cochlear damage
Petrous fracture, nerve damage

INFECTIOUS
Typhus
Viral illnesses, especially mumps, but also as sequel of measles,
    pertussis, varicella, mononucleosis
Bacterial meningitis
Tuberculosis
Lues (congenital or acquired)

NEOPLASMS
Cerebellopontine angle tumors (acoustic neuroma, meningioma,
    cholesteatoma)

UNKNOWN
Same as vertigo

TABLE 13

Localization of Hearing Defects

Weber: a lateralized Weber means either a conductive loss in the lateralized ear or a sensorineural loss in the other ear. Rinne: hearing better for bone conduction than air conduction means conductive hearing loss. Then get specific tests:

SPECIFIC TEST	CONDUCTIVE (EXTERNAL–MIDDLE EAR)	COCHLEAR (INNER EAR)	NERVE	CENTRAL
Pure-tone audiogram				
Air conduction	→	→	→	
Bone conduction		→	→	
Recruitment				
Alternate binaural loudness balance	0	+	0	0
Short-increment sensitivity index	0	+	0	0
Speech discrimination	Consistent with audiogram	Consistent with audiogram	Much worse than audiogram	Much worse than audiogram
Adaptation, abnormal tone decay	0	0	+	+
Bekesy				
Type I (superimposed continuous and intermittent tones)	+			0
Type II (continuous drops below, intermittent above 1,000 Hz)		+		
Type III (continuous tone rapidly drops as frequency increases)			+	+
Type IV (continuous constantly below, intermittent at all frequencies)			+	+
Impedance Audiometry				
Tympanometry	+	0		+
Stapedius decay	0	0	+	0

TABLE 14

Causes of Dizziness

DEGENERATIVE

Involvement of cranial nerve VIII can result in vertigo and/or deafness; tests are available to determine whether the labyrinthine system is functioning, and audiologic batteries are available to specifically locate the site of the hearing loss
  Multiple sclerosis
  Syringobulbia
  Cerebellar degenerations
  Otosclerosis

CONGENITAL

Caloric tests may be abnormal in patients with congenital deafness
  Arnold-Chiari syndrome
  Platybasia
  Basilar impression

TOXIC/METABOLIC

  Dilantin
  Barbiturates
  Streptomycin
  Kanamycin
  Neomycin
  Gentamicin
  Quinine
  Alcohol
  Lead
  Arsenic
  Thiamine deficiency (beriberi)
  Niacin deficiency (pellagra)
  Hyperventilation
  Hypothyroidism
  Hypoglycemia

VASCULAR

  Vertebrobasilar insufficiency
  Periarteritis nodosa (Cogan's syndrome of interstitial keratitis and
    audiovestibular symptoms)
  Brainstem ischemia, as in distribution of posterior inferior
    cerebellar artery
  Cerebellar hemorrhage
  Nerve (occlusion of internal auditory artery)
  Hypertension
  Hypotension of any etiology
  Migraine
  Aneurysm
  Tortuous vessels

TRAUMATIC

  Labyrinthine disruption
  Petrous fractures, nerve damage

TABLE 14 (CONT.)

INFECTIOUS
Otitis media
Labyrinthitis
Viral illness
Abscess, cerebellar
Tuberculous
Syphilis
Arachnoiditis
Bacterial meningitis (usually vertigo subsides when patient
  becomes ambulatory)

NEOPLASTIC
Cerebellopontine angle tumor (infrequent complaint): acoustic neuroma,
  meningioma, cholesteatoma
Cerebellar astrocytoma, hemangioma, metastatic
Glomus jugulare of middle ear

OTHER
Vestibular neuronitis (? toxic, degenerative, viral); benign postural vertigo (? viral);
  Meniere's syndrome; sarcoidosis; Vogt-Koyanagi-Harada syndrome; temporal
  lobe epilepsy; Paget's disease; impacted cerumen

TABLE 15

Differentiating Features of Some Common Causes of Dizziness

CAUSE OF DIZZINESS	TIME COURSE OF ATTACK	TYPE OF VERTIGO	CALORIC RESPONSE	ASSOCIATED SYMPTOMS	DEAFNESS	TINNITUS	VERTIGO RELATED TO HEAD POSITION
Meniere's syndrome	Minutes to 24 hours	Severe, paroxysmal; long remissions	Abnormal	Nausea, vomiting, falling, past pointing, nystagmus	Low tone, increased in attacks; progressive; helped by hearing aid	+ low tone	Patient tends to hold head still
Vestibular neuronitis	5–10 days	Severe and constant early with slow decline in symptoms over days; long remissions	Abnormal	Nausea, vomiting, nystagmus—after rotatory	No	No	Patient tends to hold head still
Benign positional vertigo	5–15 sec after position change	Severe; remissions	Normal	Preceding viral illness	No	No	Specific
Vertebrobasilar insufficiency	Seconds	Severe, recurrent	Usually normal	Numbness, dysarthria, diplopia, drop attacks, weakness	Rare	No	No
CPA tumor	Mild imbalance that may improve	Rarely true vertigo	Abnormal	Other cranial nerve dysfunction, late increased intracranial pressure	Progressive of all frequencies; not helped by amplification	+	Rarely
Psychogenic cause	Attack lasts an "instant" but occurs frequently	Ill-defined	Normal	Variable	Variable	Variable	Variable

TABLE 16

Types of Nystagmus

Physiologic nystagmus: present in normal individuals

End point: when the fixated target can be seen by only one eye
Medication-induced: diphenyl hydantoin, alcohol antihistamines and others.
Rotational: postrotational nystagmus has the fast phase opposite to the direction of
rotation
Optokinetic calorics: cold water with head tilted back 60° produces a slow phase toward
the irrigated ear and fast phase away; bilateral stimulation causes slow down gaze and
fast up phase

Vestibular

Ablative lesions cause nystagmus to the opposite side (similar to the effects of
cold calorics that decrease the resting discharge of the vestibular apparatus on the
side stimulated), falling to same side and past pointing on the same side. Blurring of
vision (not diplopia), severe vertigo, and illusion of a moving environment are present.
Acute labyrinthitis can be irritative with a reversal of the above. The nystagmus is
usually horizontal, but may be rotatory. Rotatory nystagmus means vestibular system
disease—characteristically vestibular nuclei. Although most of the causes of dizziness
(see Table 14) can produce at least transient nystagmus, the most common offenders
are the following: Meniere's disease, vestibular neuronitis, benign positional vertigo,
multiple sclerosis, and posterior fossa neoplasms.

Central nystagmus, specific localizing types:

Dissociated: nystagmus only of the abducting eye from a lesion of the medial longi-
tudinal fasciculus; multiple sclerosis in young and vascular disease in elderly
Vertical: brainstem, although most common cause is medication
Down-beating, especially on lateral and down gaze: lesion in region of the foramen
magnum, eg, Arnold-Chiari malformation, high cervical meningioma
Seesaw: one eye rising as the other falls, usually with bitemporal hemianopsia from a
long-standing lesion near optic chiasm.
Periodic alternating: spontaneous direction changes from vestibular nuclear lesion
Rotatory: vestibular nucleus (can be peripheral)
Retractorius: often associated with convergence nystagmus (sylvian aqueduct lesion)
Monocular: usually brainstem
Gaze paretic: causes nystagmus when one attempts to look in the direction of a gaze
paresis of either cerebral or brainstem origin
Epileptic: as part of the adversive head and eye deviation from a frontal eye field focus

Pendular nystagmus

Congenital: hereditary or birth trauma
Central visual loss: before age 2 years
Spasmus nutans

Other eye movements

Opsoclonus: chaotic, often dissociated, eye movements
Ocular dysmetria
Ocular flutter
Wandering movements of the blind

TABLE 17

Diseases Affecting the Lower Four Cranial Nerves

NEOPLASMS
   Glomus jugulare
   Lymphoma-leukemia
   Neurinoma
   Meningioma
   Chondroma
   Nasopharyngeal neoplasm

VASCULAR DISEASE
   Jugular vein thrombophlebitis

INFECTIONS
   Arachnoiditis
      Bacterial
      Tuberculous
      Fungal
      Syphilitic
   Abscess
   Otitic infection

TRAUMA

OTHER
   Sarcoidosis
   Basilar impression
   Syringobulbia
   Amyotrophic lateral sclerosis

10
Stiff Neck

The patient found to have a stiff neck on examination represents an important differential diagnostic problem. Many elderly patients, children with acute febrile illnesses, and chronically ill patients may have stiff neck that does not represent treatable central nervous system involvement. A patient with tonsillar herniation may have neck stiffness, and a spinal tap could represent a grave danger. However, the finding of Kernig's sign or Brudzinski's sign of meningeal irritation indicates infectious, neoplastic, or chemical inflammation of the meninges, and a lumbar puncture must be done to define the etiology. Table 1 is a list of the cerebrospinal fluid findings that may be useful for distinguishing these etiologies and for guiding further evaluation. Table 2 lists the most common causes of depressed CSF glucose, and Table 3 lists the most common causes of lymphocytosis.

If the cerebrospinal fluid parameters indicate an acute bacterial meningitis, then therapy must be initiated before cultures become positive. Following cerebrospinal fluid, blood, and sputum cultures, chest, skull, and sinus films, and appropriate stains, the most likely correct antibiotic must be started, and no change should be made unless clinical deterioration or culture results make change necessary. If the patient does not have a communication between skin and subarachnoid space, does not have cancer, and is not immunosuppressed, then the antibiotic is chosen on the basis of age, as indicated in Table 4.

The clinician should confirm the appropriate antibiotic with cultures and continue therapy for 10 to 14 days. There is no need to repeat lumbar puncture until the end of a therapeutic course, unless the clinical picture is one of deterioration.

A difficult problem arises when the patient has depressed consciousness and focal neurologic deficits when first seen. Although this may result from a vasculitis secondary to the meningitis, it may represent an abscess with rupture to the ventricle or an empyema, both making lumbar puncture dangerous. If the patient is seriously ill, time is critical, and it is best to initiate antibiotics after blood and sputum cultures, but without lumbar puncture. Brain scan, EEG, CAT scan, and/or angiography can then be done to define the process. A mass lesion will require surgical intervention. Clearly each patient should be individualized, but a good general approach is outlined in the Table 5 flowchart.

Often with a history of sudden onset of headache, depressed consciousness, and a stiff neck on examination, the cerebrospinal fluid will be bloody. The differentiation from a traumatic tap is not difficult if the first and fourth tubes of fluid have similar cell counts and the supernatant is xanthochromic, especially after a few hours. If there is no history of trauma, then a saccular aneurysm is the most likely diagnosis. Prior to age 30 years, especially ages 15 to 20 years, arteriovenous malformations cause subarachnoid hemorrhage almost as frequently. Taking all ages into consideration, the differential for nontraumatic subarachnoid hemorrhage is as follows:

Aneurysm	51%
Hypertensive-arteriosclerotic	15%
Arteriovenous malformation	6%
Miscellaneous (eg, anticoagulation, dyscrasias, vasculitis)	6%
Unknown	22%

An aneurysmal bleed usually occurs in a previously asymptomatic individual, although an internal carotid posterior communicating aneurysm can produce palsy of cranial nerve III.

The natural history of aneurysmal subarachnoid hemorrhage reveals a high early mortality followed by increasing risk until about 2 to 3 weeks post bleed, with relatively good prognosis if the patient survives in good clinical condition past this period. The high mortality following the very early deaths can be attributed largely to rebleeding. It seems logical that therapy should be aimed at interrupting the natural history of high rebleeding during the 3- to 11-day period after the initial bleed. Unfortunately, to this date no large controlled series has shown that early surgery improves mortality over medical therapy. In addition, if the patient does survive for 3 weeks in good clinical condition, he is likely to do well whether or not surgery is performed. At this time it appears that bedrest and antifibrinolytic therapy are the best early therapy, with a decision regarding surgery being delayed until 14 days have passed, and then being based on the expertise of available neurologic surgery and the patient's clinical state. A decision regarding surgery for other common hemorrhagic conditions must be individually determined. However, of the intracerebral hematomas, only cerebellar hemorrhage should be routinely treated surgically. Arteriovenous malformations may be considered operable for intractable seizures or if massive intracerebral hemorrhage has occurred, but in general, surgical mortality is not unlike the mortality inflicted by the disease itself. The evaluation of a suspected hemorrhage is outlined in Table 6; also see Chapter 11 (Apoplexy).

TABLE 1

Cerebrospinal Fluid Findings in Stiff Neck

DISEASE	OPENING PRESSURE (mm OF WATER) SPINAL FLUID HORIZONTAL POSITION	APPEARANCE	CELLS (per mm³)	PROTEIN (mg/100 ml)	SUGAR (mg/100 ml)	COMMENTS
Lumbar puncture (normal)	<180	Clear, colorless	0–5	15–45	50–75	Sugar applies to fasting non-febrile individuals
Traumatic tap	Normal	Blood-tinged or bloody	Many red blood cells; 1 white cell for every 1,000 RBC	50–70	Normal	Progressively less bloody in consecutive tubes; supernatant clear
Meningism	200–500	Normal	Normal	5–45	50–100	Excess of clear fluid with low protein content
Purulent meningitis	200–800	Cloudy	500–20,000, chiefly polymorphonuclear leukocytes	100–1,000	Decreased	Sugar usually falls rapidly; organisms should be searched for in clot or sediment; culture positive
Tuberculous meningitis	200–800	Mild xanthochromia, fibrin web	50–300 mononuclears	60–700	Decreased	Excess fluid; polymorphonuclear leukocytes may be found early; progressive fall in sugar value; tubercle bacilli may be found in clot or sediment; culture positive

TABLE 1 (CONT.)

DISEASE	OPENING PRESSURE (mm OF WATER) SPINAL FLUID HORIZONTAL POSITION	APPEARANCE	CELLS (per mm)	PROTEIN (mg/100 ml)	SUGAR (mg/100ml)	COMMENTS
Fungal meningitis (especially cryptococcal)	Normal to slightly increased	Clear, mildly cloudy, or slightly xanthochromic	10–500, mostly monocytes	50–600	Decreased	India ink preparation for cryptococci; gamma globulin may be elevated; culture positive; antigen test may be positive
Viral meningo-encephalitis	Normal	Clear, colorless	30–350, chiefly mononuclears	40–80	Normal	Low sugar has been reported in mumps, herpes simplex, eastern equine
Acute syphilitic meningitis	150–300	Clear, slight opalescence	300–2,000 mononuclears	50–400	Normal	Serologic test nearly always strongly positive; elevated gamma globulin
Tertiary central nervous system lues	Normal	Clear	10–40 mononuclears	50–100	Normal	Positive serologic test for syphilis in nearly 100% of untreated paretics, but negative tests in many tabetics; elevated gamma globulin
Brain abscess	200–800	Clear, colorless; may be xanthochromic	30–100 polymorphonuclears when not encapsulated; 30–100 monocytes when encapsulated	50–400	Normal	Polymorphonuclears nearly always present early; similar picture in sinus thrombosis and extradural abscess; in later stages mononuclears predominate

Condition						
Sarcoidosis	Normal to slightly increased	Clear		Normal to 500	Decreased	Negative cell block
Multiple sclerosis (clinically active)	Normal	Normal	5–50 mononuclears	20–70	Normal	Elevated gamma globulin
Cerebral thrombosis	150–250	Clear or yellow	Usually normal; may have 50–75 mononuclears	60–80	Normal	Pleocytosis when softening approaches surface or ventricular system
Brain tumor	150–500	Clear or yellow	Usually normal; may have 50–300 mononuclears	20–150	Normal	Pleocytosis most likely when tumor invades ventricular system or surface of brain
Meningeal carcinomatosis	Normal to slightly increased	Clear but may be mucinous		Normal to 500	Decreased	Malignant cells in cell block
Subarachnoid or ventricular hemorrhage	150–250	Bloody; supernatant yellow	Equal numbers of RBC's in 1st and 4th tubes; larger numbers of WBC's secondary to meningeal inflammation	100–800	Normal	Normal sugar gradually decreases after 10 days; protein value increases
Froin's syndrome	20–100	Deep yellow, clear, massive coagulation	Normal	Up to 6,000	Normal	Partial block may produce increase in spinal fluid protein

TABLE 2

Causes of Depressed Cerebrospinal Fluid Glucose*

INFECTIONS
Bacterial
Fungal
Tuberculous
Some viral agents
  Mumps
  Herpes simplex
  Eastern equine encephalitis
Amebic (*Naegleria* species)
Acute syphilitic meningitis (rare)

NEOPLASTIC DISEASE
Gliomas
Melanoma
Sarcoma
Lymphoma-leukemia
Meningeal carcinomatosis

VASCULAR DISEASE
Subarachnoid hemorrhage

OTHER
Sarcoidosis
Reaction to cisternography (RISA)
Acute necrotizing hemorrhagic encephalopathy
Brain death

This must always be judged in relation to a simultaneous blood sample. Normal fasting cerebrospinal fluid glucose is approximately 70% of serum glucose.

TABLE 3

Causes of Cerebrospinal Fluid Lymphocytosis

INFECTIONS
  Partially treated bacterial meningitis
  Abscess (epidural, subdural, brain)
  Listeria mónocytogenes
  Brucellosis
  Viral
  Tuberculous
  Fungal
  Spirochetal
  Protozoan

DEMYELINATING

VASCULAR
  Venous thrombosis
  Arteritis
  Arterial thrombosis or embolism
  Subarachnoid hemorrhage, clearing

NEOPLASTIC
  Adjacent to ventricles or subarachnoid space
  Meningeal neoplasia

TOXIC
  Therapeutic–diagnostic
    Lumbar puncture
    Myelography
    Pneumoencephalography
    Spinal anesthesia
    RISA cisternography
    Intrathecal medications
  Heavy metals (eg, lead)

OTHER
  Sarcoidosis
  Behçet's syndrome
  Vogt-Koyanagi syndrome
  Harada's syndrome
  Mollaret's meningitis

TABLE 4

Antibiotic Treatment for Bacterial Meningitis

AGE	MOST COMMON ORGANISM	ANTIBIOTIC
Premature–2 months	*Escherichia coli* *Streptococcus* (Group B) *Listeria monocytogenes* *Diplococcus pneumoniae*	Ampicillin, 200–400 mg/kg/day intravenously in divided doses every 4 hours, and gentamicin, 6 mg/kg/day intravenously in divided doses every 8 hours
2 months–10 years	*Haemophilus influenzae*	Ampicillin, 200–400 mg/kg/day intravenously in divided doses every 4 hours; if ampicillin-resistant strains have been locally reported, then chloramphenicol, 100 mg/kg/day in divided doses every 6 hours for children and adults, 25 mg/kg/day for infants
10–30 years	*Neisseria meningitidis*	Penicillin G, 12–20 million IU/day in divided doses intravenously
30 years and older	*Diplococcus pneumoniae*	Penicillin G, 12–20 million IU/day in divided doses intravenously

TABLE 5

Evaluation of Probable Meningitis

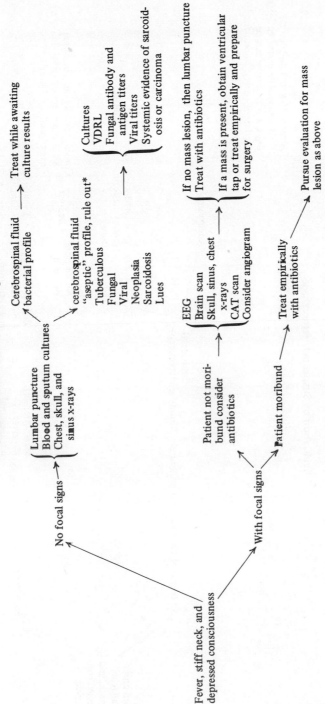

Fever, stiff neck, and depressed consciousness

→ No focal signs →
- Lumbar puncture
- Blood and sputum cultures
- Chest, skull, and sinus x-rays

→ Cerebrospinal fluid bacterial profile → Treat while awaiting culture results

→ cerebrospinal fluid "aseptic" profile, rule out*
- Tuberculous
- Fungal
- Viral
- Neoplasia
- Sarcoidosis
- Lues

→
- Cultures
- VDRL
- Fungal antibody and antigen titers
- Viral titers
- Systemic evidence of sarcoidosis or carcinoma

→ With focal signs →

Patient not moribund consider antibiotics →
- EEG
- Brain scan
- Skull, sinus, chest x-rays
- CAT scan
- Consider angiogram

→ If no mass lesion, then lumbar puncture Treat with antibiotics

If a mass is present, obtain ventricular tap or treat empirically and prepare for surgery

Patient moribund → Treat empirically with antibiotics → Pursue evaluation for mass lesion as above

*It may be worthwhile to treat with antibiotics (see Table 4) until bacterial cultures negative. If one suspects tuberculosis, then treatment should be initiated prior to obtaining culture results.

199

TABLE 6

Evaluation of Suspected Hemorrhage

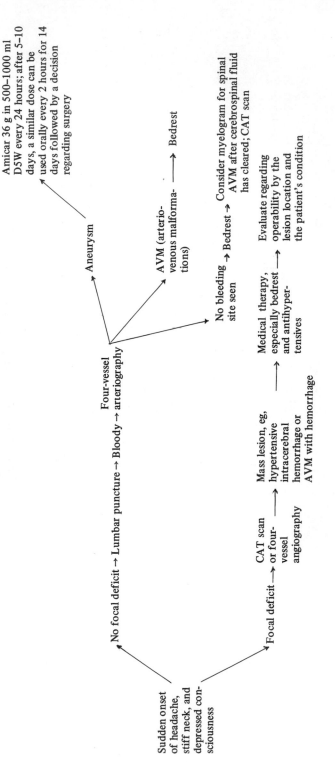

Sudden onset of headache, stiff neck, and depressed consciousness

No focal deficit → Lumbar puncture → Bloody → Four-vessel arteriography

Aneurysm → Amicar 36 g in 500–1000 ml D5W every 24 hours; after 5–10 days, a similar dose can be used orally every 2 hours for 14 days followed by a decision regarding surgery

AVM (arteriovenous malformations) → Bedrest

No bleeding site seen → Bedrest → Consider myelogram for spinal AVM after cerebrospinal fluid has cleared; CAT scan

Focal deficit → CAT scan or four-vessel angiography → Mass lesion, eg, hypertensive intracerebral hemorrhage or AVM with hemorrhage → Medical therapy, especially bedrest and antihypertensives → Evaluate regarding operability by the lesion location and the patient's condition

11
Apoplexy

The sudden onset of a neurologic defect is frequently called apoplexy or stroke. Although a stroke is thought of as an untreatable disease, many of the diseases that produce a stroke can and should be treated after the proper diagnosis is made. A differential diagnosis of stroke can be found in Table 1. The differential diagnosis between hemorrhage and infarction can be difficult (Table 2). Frequently, laboratory studies are needed. This differential is important, because frequently with infarction (especially embolization) one wants to anticoagulate the patient. If the patient hemorrhaged, anticoagulation would be devastating. In addition, since hemorrhage often needs surgical intervention, it is again important to separate hemorrhage from infarction. The differential diagnosis between intracerebral and subarachnoid hemorrhage can be found in Table 3. Table 4 contains the clinical signs and recommended treatment of the various causes of hemorrhage. Table 5 contains the differential diagnosis between embolus and thrombosis, and Table 6 contains the clinical signs and recommended treatment of the various causes of infarction.

TABLE 1

Etiology of Stroke

HEMORRHAGE

Intracerebral

Hypertensive
  Putamen
  Thalamus
  Pons
  Cerebellum
Bleeding Disorders
Trauma
AVM
Aneurysm (especially MCA)

Subarachnoid

Aneurysm
  Posterior communicating
  Anterior communicating
  Middle cerebral artery
  Carotid
  Vertebral basilar
AVM
Trauma
Bleeding Disorder

INFARCTION

Embolus
Cardiac
  Arrhythmia
  Vascular
  Myocardial infarction
  Infection
Paradoxic
Great Vessel
Atrial Myxoma

Thrombosis
Athrosclerotic
  Middle cerebral artery
  Anterior cerebral artery
  Posterior cerebral artery
  Vertebral basilar

Other
Vasculitis
  SLE
  Polyarteritis
  Temporal arteritis
  Other
Sickle Cell Disease
Hypercoagulation States
Hyperviscosity States

TABLE 2

Differential Diagnosis between Hemorrhage and Infarction

HEMORRHAGE	INFARCTION
Usually no prior warning	May have prior warning or may have stuttering onset
May be associated with loss of consciousness	Except with basilar thrombosis, loss of consciousness unusual at onset
Cortical defects uncommon; can be seen with aneurysm and AVM; seizures more common	Cortical defects (ie, aphasia) common; seizure uncommon
May have stiff neck	Stiff neck rare
May have subhyloid hemorrhages and papilledema	Papilledema rare
Skull films may show shifted pineal	Skull films show midline pineal
Computerized tomography may show intracerebral mass compatible with hemorrhage (increased density with intracerebral hemorrhage, and may be normal with subarachnoid hemorrhage)	CT may show changes compatible with infarction
Arteriogram (usually the definitive study) may show intrahemispheric mass, aneurysm, or AVM	Arteriogram may show occlusion or meniscus or evidence of vasculitis
Lumbar puncture will show blood and xanthochromia	Lumbar puncture will usually be normal, may have WBC's; with emboli there may be RBC's

TABLE 3

Differential Diagnosis Between Intracerebral and Subarachnoid Hemorrhage

INTRACEREBRAL HEMORRHAGE	SUBARACHNOID HEMORRHAGE
Focal signs frequent	Focal signs less frequent; however, nerve III palsy frequent
Stiff neck less prominent	Stiff neck prominent
CT shows mass effect	CT usually without mass effect
LP may be without blood (20%), may have small amount of blood, or may be grossly bloody	LP grossly bloody with xanthochromic fluid
Arteriogram shows mass effect	Arteriogram shows aneurysm, AV malformation

TABLE 4

Differential Diagnosis of Hemorrhages

ETIOLOGY	SYMPTOMS	LABORATORY	TREATMENT
Hypertensive			
Putamenal	Contralateral hemiplegia, hemianesthesia, hemianopsia, and deviation of eyes toward the lesion	CT, arteriogram, blood studies	Reduce blood pressure; ? steroids; supportive
Thalamic	Contralateral hemiparesis, hemianesthesia, hemianopsia, eyes deviated downward, with small or midsized unreactive pupils	Same as above	Reduce blood pressure; ? steroids; supportive
Pontine	Rapid-onset coma, pinpoint pupils, hyperventilation, loss of reflex eye movements, bilateral pyramidal tract signs	Same as above	Reduce blood pressure; ? steroids; supportive
Cerebellar	Dizziness, nausea, and vomiting; cerebellar signs (not always present); eye deviation or VI nerve palsy; decreased consciousness	Same as above (carotid arteriography not sufficient)	Surgical decompression; reduce blood pressure; ? steroids
Blood Disorders	Depend on location of bleed; systemic signs	Hematology studies	Treat underlying bleeding disorder; surgical decompression
Aneurysm	Clinically, these may be difficult to separate; internal carotid may produce nasal field defect; posterior communicating aneurysms may present with III nerve palsy; anterior communicating aneurysms may produce vigilant coma, and a transcortical motor aphasia; middle cerebral artery aneurysm may produce hemiparesis, aphasia	Arteriography	Reduce blood pressure; antifibrinolytic therapy;? surgery
AV Malformation	Bruit may be audible, may produce local signs depending on location	Arteriogram	Reduce blood pressure; rest; ? surgery

TABLE 5

Differential Diagnosis between Embolus and Thrombosis

EMBOLUS	THROMBOSIS
Onset rapid, clearing may be rapid, other organs may be involved	Frequently stuttering onset
Seizure more frequent	Seizures less frequent
Spinal fluid may show blood or xanthochromia	Spinal fluid without blood or xanthochromia
Arteriogram may show meniscus	Arteriogram shows occlusion
Underlying heart disease (ie, valvular, myocardial infarction)	May also have evidence of ASHD

TABLE 6

Differential Diagnosis and Treatment of Infarction

ETIOLOGY	SIGNS AND SYMPTOMS	LABORATORY	TREATMENT
Thrombosis			
Internal carotid	Hemiparesis, hemianesthesia, hemianopsia, aphasia (global or mixed transcortical), neglect	Serum lipids; GTT; noninvasive studies (ie, CT)	Supportive; if hypertensive, blood pressure must be reduced gradually; ? dextran; ? glycerol
Middle cerebral	Hemiparesis (arm and face > leg), hemianopsia, cortical signs (see Chapter 6), cortical sensory defect	Same as above	Same as above
Anterior cerebral	Hemiparesis (leg > arm), grasp, callosal disconnection syndrome	Same as above	Same as above
Posterior cerebral	Hemianopsia, defective memory, alexia without agraphia	Same as above	Same as above
Vertebral basilar	Cranial nerve abnormality, cerebellar signs, weakness, sensory signs (see Chapter 9, Table 2)	Same as above	Same as above
Embolus	Has localization similar to thrombosis	Cardiac evaluation	Anticoagulation
Other (ie, vasculitis and sickle cell)	Similar to above; however, there may also be systemic signs	Sedimentation rate, hematologic studies, LE prep, ANA, temporal artery biopsy, hemoglobin electrophoresis	Treat underlying disease

12
Cerebral Palsy and Hypotonia of Infancy

As a general term, cerebral palsy implies any fixed upper motor neuron deficit attributable (by custom) to a perinatal insult. Among the etiologies commonly linked with cerebral palsy are perinatal anoxia, cerebral hemorrhage, arterial and venous thromboses, and kernicterus. However, to this must be added anything that might result in a motor deficit (see causes of static encephalopathy in Chapter 14). The premature infant is much more vulnerable than is the full-term child. Certainly, depending on the extent and location of this damage, associated disturbances of visual, auditory, and sensory function as well as intellectual capacity will also limit the patient's capabilities. For example, significant involvement of cortical sensory function will severely limit the use of the limb regardless of the efforts (physical therapy, surgery, drugs) provided to restore motor function. Of greatest importance is the need to affirm the deficit as being fixed rather than progressive, which would thereby imply an ongoing disease.

In Table 1 are listed the terms used to identify these motor problems, their clinical features, the most commonly found pathology, and treatment approaches.

Muscle tone is dependent on the physical interactions of the muscle fiber and its tendon attachments, as well as the physiologic states of the controlling central and peripheral nervous systems. A decrease in tone (hypotonia) characteristically occurs for a period immediately following any sort of abrupt insult of significant degree to the motor controlling pathways in the nervous system (eg, spinal shock). It is also evident during the early phase of certain progressive degenerative diseases of infancy and as a consequence of perinatal insults (cerebral palsy) where the cerebellum as well as other portions of the motor system have been involved. Depending on the progression of the degenerative disease and the extent of damage in the child with cerebral palsy, the hypotonic state becomes changed within months to years, and spasticity, rigidity, or dystonic posturing may appear.

Circumstances in which hypotonia is persistent are conditions associated primarily with dysfunction of the peripheral nervous system (lower motor neuron, nerve, muscle). In addition, however, selective involvement of the posterior columns or root entry zone of the spinal cord, cerebellum, or parietal lobe may be manifested by hypotonia in the corresponding extremities.

Table 2 lists those conditions in which, during the early period of insult, hypotonia is evident, and Table 3 provides a list of those conditions where persistent hypotonia exists.

TABLE 1

Types of Cerebral Palsy

CLASSIFICATION	CLINICAL PRESENTATION	PATHOLOGY	TREATMENT
Spastic			
Quadriplegia	Four limbs weak, spastic, hyperreflexia; pathologic reflexes; poor trunk control; mental retardation profound	Premature birth; periventricular hemorrhage; subcortical or cortical infarct; diffuse anoxic insult	Physical therapy; braces and orthopedic procedures to limit deformities; drug therapy for spasticity is ineffective
Diplegia	Lower extremities more severely affected than upper (spastic, proximal weakness, hyperreflexia, pathologic reflexes); mental retardation	Premature birth; periventricular leukomalacia or hemorrhage	As above
Hemiplegia	One-sided involvement; face usually unaffected; spastic, distal upper extremity and proximal lower extremity weakness most evident; hyperreflexia; pathologic reflexes; mentally normal	Contralateral infarct	As above
Monoplegia	Upper or lower extremity on one side of body significantly more affected than associated ipsilateral limb with respect to weakness and spasticity; mentally normal	Contralateral infarct	As above

Type	Clinical Features	Etiology	Therapy
Triplegia	Only one of four limbs seemingly unaffected by weakness, spasticity, hyperreflexia, and pathologic reflexes; mental retardation	Anoxic; vascular or periventricular hemorrhage	As above
Ataxic	Trunk and extremity ataxia, dyssynergia, dysmetria, dysdiadochokinesia; mental retardation	Anoxic; cerebral and cerebellar insult	Gait training; speech therapy, activities of daily living
Dyskinetic (Choreoathetosis and dystonia)	Involuntary movements of limbs and trunk observed spontaneously as well as after voluntary effort; mentally retarded; often deaf	Anoxic or kernicteric basal ganglia involvement	Activities of daily living, speech and hearing therapy
Atonic Diplegia	Hypotonic quadriparetic with greatest involvement in lower extremities; associated hyperreflexia, poor trunk control, becoming spastic after 2 or 3 years; mentally retarded	Anoxic; cerebral and cerebellar insults	As above
Mixed	Combinations of above, eg, spastic-ataxic		

TABLE 2

Causes of Temporary Hypotonia

SPINAL SHOCK (NEURAL DIASCHISIS)
Trauma to brain or cord
Severe vascular insult and hemorrhage
Anoxia
Overwhelming nervous system infection or sepsis

DRUG OVERDOSAGE
Anticonvulsants
Narcotics
Tranquilizers
Soporifics
Neuromuscular agents

DEGENERATIVE DISEASES (see Chap. 14)
Cerebrohepatorenal syndrome
Urea cycle enzyme deficiency states (aminoacidopathy)
Gangliosidoses (lipid storage diseases)
Krabbe's disease
Metachromatic leukodystrophy
Infantile neuroaxonal dystrophy

PERINATAL INSULT (CEREBRAL PALSY) (see Chap. 15)
Kernicterus
Anoxic damage to cerebellum plus other areas

TABLE 3

Causes of Permanent Hypotonia

CENTRAL NERVOUS SYSTEM
Parietal lobe disease
Cerebellar disease (see Chap. 4)
    Cerebellar ataxia (residuum of acute infection)
    Cerebellar degenerative diseases
Posterior column and root entry zone disease (see Chap. 2)
    Tabes dorsalis

PERIPHERAL NERVOUS SYSTEM AND MUSCLE
Anterior horn cell (see Chap. 2)
    Polio
    Werdnig-Hoffmann disease
    Kugelberg-Welander-Wohlfahrt disease
    Arthrogryposis
Peripheral nerve (see Chap. 2 and 3)
    Polyneuropathy (acquired and genetic)
    Dysautonomia
Myasthenic states (see Chap. 2)
Myopathies and myositis (see Chap. 2)

13
Abnormal Head Size

Unusual head size or shape may reflect underlying brain abnormality, or it may represent a benign process related to genetic factors. For example, in certain families large heads (macrocrania) or small heads (microcrania) may be unassociated with any evidence of brain dysfunction.

PREMATURE SUTURE CLOSURE

Premature closure of a cranial suture may result in a misshapen head, but most often no cerebral problem exists. Table 1 lists the types of skull abnormalities resulting from premature suture closure.

MACROCRANIA

In the infant in whom there is a question of excessive head size, serial measurements compared against standard percentiles for age will often clarify the need for further investigation. In essence, the pathologic processes resulting in macrocrania are those that interfere with the free flow of CSF in the cranium, thus causing proximal ventricular dilatation (hydrocephalus), and those that because of mass effect cause an expansion of the cranial vault. Table 2 lists the studies important in ascertaining the etiology of macrocrania. Table 3 lists the more common causes of macrocrania requiring investigation and definitive treatment.

MICROCRANIA

Microcrania or small head can likewise be determined first by comparing size against standards. It has been accepted that a head circumference more than 2 standard deviations below the mean is microcephalic. Table 4 lists the more common causes of microcephaly. It should be appreciated that any postulated cerebral insult can result in secondary microcephaly, because damaged brain does not grow to stimulate skull growth.

TABLE 1

Types of Premature Suture Closure

SUTURE CLOSURE	SHAPE	COMMENT
Sagittal	Enlarged anteroposterior (A-P) and decreased transverse size	Benign (surgery for cosmetics); may result from previous trauma inciting closure
Bilateral coronal	Shortened A-P dimension with flattened occiput	Benign
Sagittal and bilateral coronal	High, narrow skull	Hearing impaired; intracranial hypertension
Unilateral coronal or lambdoid	Skewed shape	Benign
Metopic	Prominent midforehead ridge	Benign
Bilateral coronal hypertelorism and prognathism Hypoplastic maxilla Exophthalmos (Crouzon's syndrome)	Shortened A-P dimension with hypoplastic maxilla and exophthalmos Hypertelorism Prognathism	Progressive visual loss and intracranial hypertension
Acrocephaly syndactyly (eg, Apert's syndrome)	Shortened A-P dimension with hypertelorism and prognathism	Usually retarded

TABLE 2

Etiology of Macrocrania

CONGENITAL

Hydrocephalus
  Aqueductal stenosis
    Developmental
    Postinfectious
      Toxoplasmosis
      Cytomegalic inclusion disease
      Rubella
      Syphilis
    Vein of Galen malformation
    Associated syndromes: Arnold-Chiari, basilar impression, Klippel-Feil
  Obstruction of foramina of Luschka and Magendie
    Dandy-Walker syndrome
    Cyst
  Communicating hydrocephalus
    Arachnoiditis (postinfectious)
    Achondroplasia
    Unknown

Hydranencephaly

Porencephaly

Other (large brain)
  Neurocutaneous syndrome (von Recklinghausen's neurofibromatosis)
  Cerebral gigantism
  Maternal ingestion of drugs (Aminopterin)

ACQUIRED

Hydrocephalus
  Postinfectious
    Pyogenic (arachnoiditis)
    Mumps (aqueductal stenosis)
  Posttraumatic hemorrhage blocking aqueduct or causing arachnoiditis
  Neoplasm
    Intraventricular
    Compression of ventricle or aqueduct
      Brainstem
      Cerebellar
      Suprasellar
      Quadrigeminal plate
      Extraaxial posterior fossa mass
    Subarachnoid block
      Leukemia
      Lymphoma

Subdural fluid
  Posttraumatic hematoma
  Infection
    Subdural empyema
    Subdural effusion
  Post pneumoencephalography

TABLE 2 (CONT'D.)

Intracerebral mass effect
  Hemispheric neoplasm or abscess

Intrinsic brain disease
  Canavan's spongy degeneration
  Alexander's disease
  Krabbe's disease
  Mucopolysaccharidoses
  Ganglioside storage diseases

Extracerebral mass
  Leptomeningeal cyst

TABLE 3

Investigative Techniques for Macrocrania

INSPECTION
  Plotting measurement against age, chest circumference, weight, length
  Asymmetries and ridges
  Prominence of vascular pattern
  Palpation of anterior fontanelle and elsewhere
  Listening for bruits
  Mobility of head on neck

LABORATORY
  X-rays (skull, chest)
  Computerized axial tomography
  Arteriography (significant cranial bruit, enlarged heart)
  Viral antibody titers
  Toxoplasmosis serum antibody levels
  Lumbar puncture
  Pursuit of specific tests for degenerative disease
  Subdural tap

TABLE 4

Etiology of Microcrania

GENETIC
Familial
Abnormal chromosomes
  Trisomies 21, 18, 3
  Autosomal structural changes
    46,XY translocation
    46,XY,5p
    46,XY,4p
    46,18(q-p-r)
    46,XY,13(q-r)
    46,XY,21(q-r)
    46,XY,22(q-r)
Syndromes
  Rubinstein-Taybi
  Smith-Lemli-Opitz
  Cornelia de Lange
  Hallermann-Streiff
  Prader-Willi

PRENATAL INSULT
Infection
  Toxoplasmosis
  Cytomegalovirus
  Rubella
  Herpes simplex
  Syphilis
  Other viruses
Radiation
Toxic (alcohol)
Systemic maternal disease
  Diabetes
  Chronic renal disease
  Phenylketonuria
Intrauterine problems
  Maternal systemic hypotension
  Placental insufficiencies
  Anoxia

POSTNATAL INSULT
Infection
Trauma
Anoxia
Vascular
Chronic cardiac, renal, pulmonary, gastrointestinal disease
Degenerative diseases

14
Mental Deficiency

Mental deficiency is a nonspecific term used to define the child with dementia (or amentia) who may or may not exhibit other features of neurologic impairment. Certainly the two most common groups of patients exhibiting an impairment of intellectual capacity are (1) children whose problems are related to psychosocial deprivation and (2) children whose genetic lineages have provided them an inherently limited ability.

Indeed, the diagnosis of mental deficiency is limited by demands of culture. Certain standards are established, and the individual patient is labeled, depending on his scoring on these standard parameters. For example, on traditional IQ tests normal is above 90; between 50 and 90 the child is said to be educable, and below 50 the child is considered trainable. In any event, the physician is called on to identify the cause and prognosticate if not treat. A major concern in the diagnostic evaluation is to decide (based on history and observation) whether the problem is static or is progressively worsening. The child with a less than gross static insult causing mental deficiency will continue to change in terms of his ability to adapt to his environment and will appear to improve as far as his intellectual capabilities are concerned. On the other hand, the progressive deteriorating disease will result in a worsening. This separation is sometimes difficult to establish, particularly when environmental and psychologic stresses, acquired illnesses, drugs, and seizures may modify the static process.

STATIC CAUSES OF MENTAL DEFICIENCY

Table 1 outlines the static causes for mental deficiency in childhood. The studies available to the physician to help determine the cause and define the prognosis for the patient with the presumed static insult are extensive. In certain circumstances the insult is so remote that no evidence will exist at the time of investigation. Moreover, false impressions may be gained by those seeking specific information regarding prognosis from tests that do not give the answers required; for example, a normal electroencephalogram does not exclude mental deficiency, nor does an abnormal EEG indicate that the degree of impairment is necessarily more severe.

In Table 2 are listed tests that with sufficient reason may be performed on the child based on age or clinical features on examination. Psychologic testing and vision and hearing tests are valuable studies to be performed on *all* children who have language delay or who exhibit problems in learning in a school or preschool environment. Although in certain situations an invasive neurologic procedure (arteriogram or pneumoencephalogram) may define a problem in a child with a static process who has mental deficiency (eg, arterial occlusion), these procedures are usually of little value, and they entail pain, expense, and some risk.

Within this group of children there exist many who appear peculiar or dysmorphic in terms of facies, stature, or skeleton. These children are usually thought to have polygenic disturbances, and only on the basis of the combined picture of multiple deformities can the diagnosis of a specific syndrome be established. Such conditions are listed in Table 3.

PROGRESSIVE CAUSES OF MENTAL DEFICIENCY

The so-called progressive diseases of the nervous system are manifested most often by other features of neural insult in addition to mental deficiency. Progressive disorders affecting white matter, for example, involve long motor tracts, causing early signs such as ataxia, weakness, and spasticity. On the other hand, gray matter diseases are more likely to be suspected if disturbances in mentation and seizures are evident early.

Included in this group of progressive disorders are illnesses that have been defined as metabolic in origin because a chemical change is recognized as the contributing factor. This chemical change represents a deficiency of one or another basic controlling metabolic factor in the pathway of a vital body compound. In this circumstance it is assumed that a buildup of precursor products prior to the block accounts for the clinical features of neurologic disturbance.

In many children, involvement of other organ systems is associated with the neurologic problem. Table 4 provides an outline to aid in identifying such illnesses.

Among the conditions associated with mental deficiency and progressive neurologic dysfunction are the following: (1) mass processes such as tumor, abscess, subdural hematoma, empyema, and effusion; (2) subacute and chronic infections; (3) hydrocephalus; and (4) the effects of exogenous toxins or poisons. These have been previously mentioned. Table 5 describes the progressive illnesses causing mental deficiency in infants and children that are of degenerative or metabolic origin. Salient features noted on examination are listed along with the chemical derangement, if it is known. These are subgrouped according to the general metabolic problem, as well as salient presenting problems, if such groupings exist.

Once the progressive nature of the poison is established, the laboratory studies listed in Table 6 may be considered to help make the diagnosis.

TABLE 1

Causes of Static Mental Deficiency

PRENATAL INSULT
Genetic
  Neurocutaneous disorders
  Malformations
  Chromosomal abnormalities
Infection
  Rubella
  Cytomegalovirus
  Toxoplasmosis
  Syphilis
  Herpes simplex
  Other viruses
Hypoxia
Vascular
Prematurity–postmaturity
Other maternal diseases
  Drug addiction
  Pelvic deformities
  Alcoholism
  Diabetes
  Maternal PKU
  Hypoglycemia
  Hemorrhage
  Eclampsia
  Hypothyroidism
Placental insufficiency syndromes
Kernicterus
Exogenous factors
  X-ray
  Drugs (?)
  Trauma

POSTNATAL INSULT
Trauma
Hypoxia
Infection
  Meningitis
  Encephalitis
  Hyperthermia
Metabolic
  Hypoglycemia
  Other chronic systemic illness
Idiopathic uncontrolled seizures
Vascular stroke
Exogenous factors
  Poisons (eg, lead)
  Drugs

TABLE 2

Tests for Static Causes of Mental Deficiency

PRENATAL INSULT

Genetic
  Amniotic α-fetoprotein
  Skull x-rays
  Chromosomes
  Dermatoglyphics
Infection
  Skull x-rays
  Serologic studies
Metabolic
  Thyroid function test
  Blood sugar
  Phenylalanine level (newborn)
Kernicterus
  Blood type (newborn)
  Bilirubin (newborn)

POSTNATAL INSULT

Metabolic
  Blood sugar
  Thyroid function
  Systemic disease search
  Calcium, phosphorus
Seizures
  EEG
  Anticonvulsive drug levels
Exogenous
  Lead levels and other heavy metals
  Drug survey

OPTIONAL

EEG
Skull x-rays (calcium)
Computerized axial tomography (calcium masses)
Phenylalanine metabolites in urine

TABLE 3

Dysmorphic Conditions and Chromosomal Abnormalities Associated With Static Causes of Mental Deficiency

DYSMORPHIC CONDITIONS	CHARACTERISTICS
Cerebral gigantism	Macrocranium; height and weight > 90%
Prader-Willi syndrome	Obesity, hypogenitalism, hypotonia
Pseudohypoparathyroidism	Poor tooth enamel, short stature, short fourth metacarpal, subcutaneous calcifications
Hypercalcemia, elfin facies, aortic stenosis	
Acrocephalosyndactyly syndromes	Craniosynostosis and syndactyly
Oculocerebral syndrome with hypopigmentation	Cloudy corneas; absent hair and skin pigment
Oculocerebrorenal syndrome of Lowe	Glaucoma, hypotonia, renal dysfunction
Cerebrohepatorenal syndrome	Glaucoma, hypotonia, corneal opacities, interstitial fibrosis of liver
de Lange syndrome	Hypertrophy, brows and lashes; brachycephaly; micromelia; increased body hair
Laurence-Moon-Biedl syndrome	Obesity, retinitis pigmentosa, polydactyly, hypogenitalism
Leprechaunism	Emaciation, hirsuitism, large low-set ears
Noonan's syndrome	Pulmonic stenosis, short stature, ptosis, hypertelorism, clinodactyly, cubitus valgus
Oral-facial-digital syndromes	Cleft palate, tongue, digit anomalies
Rubinstein-Taybi syndrome	Broad thumbs and toes; hypertelorism
Seckel's bird-headed dwarfism	Microcephaly, short stature, narrow face
Russell-Silver syndrome	Hemihypertrophy, short stature, elevated urinary gonadotropins
Smith-Lemli-Opitz syndrome	Syndactyly, hypospadias

CHROMOSOMAL ABNORMALITIES

Autosomal chromosomal abnormalities

Trisomy 21 (Down's syndrome: 47,XY,21+)	Microbrachycephaly, epicanthal folds, small fifth finger, hypotonia, Brushfield spots on iris
Trisomy 18 (Edwards' syndrome: 47,XY,18+)	Dolichocephaly, corneal opacity, strabismus, micrognathia, flexed with over-riding index finger, rocker-bottom feet, seizure
Trisomy 13 (Patau's syndrome: 47,XY,13+)	Microcephaly, cleft lip and palate, eye anomalies, polydactyly, deafness, seizures
Trisomy 22 (47,XY,22+)	Microcephaly, microphthalmia, down-turned mouth, micrognathia, cardiac and bone anomalies
Trisomy 8 (47,XY,8+)	Spinal dysraphism
Partial trisomy 22 (cat's-eye syndrome: 46,XY,22q+)	Vertical coloboma of iris, anal atresia, cardiac anomalies

TABLE 3 (CONT.)

Partial monosomy 5 (cri-du-chat syndrome: 46,XY,5p−)	Catlike cry, epicanthal folds, antimongoloid slant, micrognathia
Partial monosomy 4 (midline fusion defect syndrome: 46,XY,4p−)	Scalp defects, hypertelorism, cleft lip or palate, iris coloboma, hypospadias, seizures
Partial monosomies 18 (46,XY,18q−; 18p−;r[18])	Microcephaly, epicanthal folds, strabismus, hip anomalies, optic atrophy, alopecia
Partial monosomies 13 (46,XY,13q−; r[13])	Microcephaly, microphthalmia, increased incidence of retinoblastoma
Partial monosomies 21 (antimongolism: 46,XY,21q−;r[21])	Antimongoloid slant of eyelids, skeletal deformities
Partial monosomies 22 (46,XY,22q−; r[22])	Epicanthal folds, syndactyly of toes, hypotonia, microcephaly
Partial monosomies 9 (46,XY,9p−;r[9])	Misshapen pelvis, nose, ears, mouth

Sex Chromosomal

Klinefelter's syndrome (47,XXY) and variants (48,XXXY, 49,XXXXY, 47,XYY, 48,XYYX, 48,XXYY, 49,XXXYY)	Testicular dysgenesis, hypogonadism, gynecomastia, microcephaly, ocular malformations
Turner's syndrome (gonadal dysgenesis: 45,X)	Ovarian dysgenesis, short stature, shield chest, widely spaced nipples, webbed neck, short fifth metacarpal, lymphedema of dorsum of foot

TABLE 4

Signs and Symptoms of Progressive Disorders Causing Mental Deficiency

Worsening of clinical state unaccountable by:
  Psychosocial circumstances
  Drugs
  Secondary process (eg, uncontrolled epilepsy)
Occurrence of new signs and symptoms of neurologic impairment
Family history of progressive neurologic disease
Associated abnormalities
  Stature
  Skeleton
  Facies
  Skin
  Hair
  Tongue
  Vision
  Hearing
  Visceral enlargement
  Cardiac enlargement
  Odor
Other metabolic or hematologic abnormalities
  Acidosis
  Hypoglycemia
  Erythrocyte, leukocyte, platelet, or bone marrow abnormalities
Neurologic features in association with mental deficiency
  Encephalopathy (seizures, ataxia, alteration in consciousness)
  Dyskinesia
  Peripheral neuropathy
  Anterior horn cell degeneration
  Spastic weakness
  Macrocrania

TABLE 5

Causes of Progressive Mental Deficiency

CAUSE	ASSOCIATED ABNORMALITIES OR MAJOR PRESENTING PROBLEM	CHEMICAL ABNORMALITIES
Hormonal		
Hypothyroidism	Short stature; large tongue; cool, puffy, mottled skin; constipation; sparse hair; hypotonia	Absent or low thyroid hormone
Recurrent hypoglycemia Ketotic hypoglycemia Pancreatic tumor Leucine sensitivity Adrenal dysfunction	Recurrent episodes of altered consciousness or bizarre behavior	Low blood sugar
Aminoacidopathies		
Phenylketonuria	Skin and hair poorly pigmented; eczema; skin has odor of urine	Elevated serum phenylalanine, hepatic phenylalanine; hydroxylase deficiency or cofactor deficiencies
Homocystinuria	Ectopic lens; arachnodactyly; tall, thin stature; vascular occlusions; malar flush, glaucoma, pectus chest deformity	Elevated serum homocystine and methionine; cystathionine synthetase deficiency
Argininosuccinicaciduria I	Recurrent episodes of vomiting and encephalopathy (eg, seizures, ataxia, dyskinesia, confusion, coma)	Elevated argininosuccinic acid (serum and CSF argininosuccinase deficiency
Argininosuccinicaciduria II	Same as above	Elevated argininosuccinic acid, argininosuccinic acid lysase deficiency, hyperammonemia
Hyperammonemia Ornithine transcarbamylase (OTC) deficiency	Same as above	Hyperammonemia with OTC deficiency
Carbamyl phosphate synthetase (CPS) deficiency	Same as above	CPS deficiency in brain and liver

TABLE 5 (CONT.)

CAUSE	ASSOCIATED AB- NORMALITIES OR MAJOR PRESENTING PROBLEM	CHEMICAL ABNORMALITIES
Hyperammonemia (protein intolerance)	Same as argininosuccinic- aciduria I	Hyperammonemia
Ornithinemia	Same as above	Elevated serum ornithine and homocitrulline, hyperammonemia
Lysine intolerance	Same as above	Deficiency of lysine de- hydrogenase; hyperam- monemia
Maple syrup urine disease	Seizures, encephalopathy, odor of maple syrup in urine	Deficient decarboxyase of keto acids of leucine, isoleucine, valine
Intermittent maple syrup urine disease	Recurrent episodes of acidosis and encephalopathy, often during febrile states	Partial deficiencies of above enzymes
Propionicacidemia	Same as above	Elevated serum glycine propionic acid; deficient propionyl CoA carboxyl- ase
Methylmalonicacidemia	Same as above	Elevated serum methyl- malonic acid; deficient methylmalonyl CoA carboxyl mutase
Isovalericacidemia	Odor of sweaty feet and same as above	Elevated serum isovaleric acid; deficient isovaleryl CoA dehydrogenase
Pyruvate decarboxyl- ase deficiency	Same as above	Elevated serum lactic acid and pyruvic acid; hyper- alaninemia; deficient pyruvate decarboxylase
Lacticacidemia	Same as above	Elevated serum lactic acid
α-Methyl-β-hydroxy- butyricaciduria	Same as above	Elevated urine α-methyl-β- hydroxybutyric acid
Hartnup's disease	Intermittent rash and same as above	Elevated urinary indole derivatives and mono- aminomonocarboxylic amino acids

TABLE 5 (CONT.)

Hypervalinemia	Growth failure, nystagmus	Elevated serum valine, deficient valine transaminase
Hyperlysinemia	Laxity of ligaments	Elevated serum lysine, deficient lysine reductase
Sulfituria	As in homocystinuria	Increased urine cysteine, sulfite, thiosulfate; sulfite oxidase deficiency
Aspartylglycosaminuria	Grotesque face	Elevated urine aspartylglycosamine; deficient N-aspartyl-β-glycosyl-aminidase
Hyperpipecolatemia	Neuropathy, hepatomegaly, nystagmus	Elevated serum pipecolic acid; deficient pipecolate oxidase
Carbohydrate Disorders		
Fructose intolerance	Episodes of hypoglycemia after fructose ingestion; hepatomegaly, aminoaciduria	Fructosuria, deficient fructose-1-phosphate aldolase
Galactosemia	Episodes of hypoglycemia after galactose ingestion; hepatomegaly, cataract	Galactosuria, deficient galactose-1-phosphate uridyl transferase
Acid maltase deficiency (Pompe's disease, glycogen storage disease II)	Hypotonia, cardiac enlargement, tongue enlarged	Acid maltase deficiency
Lipid Storage Diseases	Progressive motor system impairment	
Tay-Sachs disease (GM$_2$ gangliosidosis type I)	Myoclonic seizures, blindness, cherry-red spot	Deficient hexosaminidase A
Sandhoff's disease (GM$_2$ gangliosidosis type II)	As in Tay-Sachs disease	Deficient hexosaminidase A and B
Neurovisceral lipidosis (GM$_1$ gangliosidosis type I)	Grotesque features, hepatomegaly, bony abnormalities (seizures without hepatomegaly in later life)	Deficient β-galactosidase A, B, and C
Gaucher's disease	Bulbar motor dysfunction, hypotonia, hepatosplenomegaly	Deficient glucose cerebrosidase

TABLE 5 (CONT.)

CAUSE	ASSOCIATED AB-NORMALITIES OR MAJOR PRESENTING PROBLEM	CHEMICAL ABNORMALITIES
Hematoside sphingo-lipodystrophy (GM$_3$ gangliosidosis de-ficiency)	Grotesque features, hepato-splenomegaly	Deficient ganglioside syn-thesis
Niemann-Pick disease	Seizures, hepatospleno-megaly, cherry-red spot	Deficient sphingomyelinase
Krabbe's disease (globoid cell leukodystrophy)	Seizures, optic atrophy, deafness	Deficient galactocerebroside β-galactosidase and cere-broside sulfotransferase
Wolman's disease (familial xanthomatosis with adrenal involvement)	Calcification of adrenal glands; hepatospleno-megaly	Acid lipase deficiency
Farber's disease (lipo-granulomatosis)	Hoarseness, joint contrac-tures, skin nodules	Deficient ceramidase
Late amaurotic idiocies (Batten-Spielmyer-Vogt, Bielchowsky, Kufs)	Retinal degeneration, seizures, ataxia	Storage of neuronal ceroid lipofuscin
Metachromatic leuko-dystrophy	Neuropathy as well as upper motor neuron dysfunc-tion; seizures; ataxia	Arylsulfatase A deficiency
Mucopolysaccharidoses and Mucolipidoses	Bony deformities and gro-tesque features, motor impairment	
Hunter's syndrome (type I)	Hepatosplenomegaly, macrocrania, corneal clouding, deafness; excre-tion in urine: heparitin sulfate (glycosamino glycans)	Deficient α-L—iduronidase
Hunter's syndrome (type II)	As in Hurler's, but less prominent; sex-linked recessive; no corneal clouding	Similar excretion pattern; deficient sulfoiduronate sulfatase
Sanfilippo A (type III)	Mild hepatosplenomegaly and bone deformities, corneal clouding	Deficient heparin N-sulfa-tase
Sanfilippo B (type III)	As in Sanfilippo A	Deficient α-acetylglucos-amidase
Fucosidosis	Enlarged heart and salivary glands	Deficient α-L-fucosidase
Mannosidosis	Hepatosplenomegaly	Deficient α-mannosidase

TABLE 5 (CONT.)

Lipomucopolysaccha-ridosis (mucolipidosis I)	Peripheral neuropathy and ataxia, cherry-red spot	
I-cell disease (muco-lipidosis II)	Hepatosplenomegaly, macroglossia	
Pseudopolydystrophy of Maroteaux and Lamy (mucolipidosis III)	Hepatosplenomegaly	
Lactosylceramidosis	Tremor, ataxia, optic atrophy, hepatospleno-megaly	Deficient lactosyl ceramide, galactosyl hydrolase
White Matter Degenerative Disease	Progressive motor impair-ment	
Canavan's disease (spongy degeneration)	Macrocrania, optic atrophy, nystagmus, seizures	
Pelizaeus-Merzbacher's disease	Nystagmus, tremor, optic atrophy, athetosis; sex-linked recessive	
Alexander's disease	Macrocrania, seizures	
Cerebrotendinosis, xanthomatosis	Cataracts, enlargement of Achilles tendons, xanthel-asma, ataxia, pseudo-bulbar palsy, palatal myo-clonus	
Schilder's disease	Cortical sensory impair-ment, ataxia, optic atrophy	
Adrenoleuko-dystrophy	Sex-linked recessive; clinical picture similar to Schilder's	
Gray Cortical Matter Degenerative Diseases	Seizures and progressive cortical motor impairment	
Alper's disease	Cortical blindness, deafness, microcephaly	
Cerebral degeneration and hepatomegaly	Hepatitis	
Kinky-hair disease	Sex-linked recessive; white, sparse, coarse, kinky hair	Low serum copper (de-ficient copper absorption)
Subacute necrotizing encephalomyelopathy (Leigh's disease)	Hypotonia, ataxia, bulbar signs, optic atrophy	Thiamine pyrophosphate inhibitor present in CSF and urine

TABLE 5 (CONT.)

CAUSE	ASSOCIATED AB-NORMALITIES OR MAJOR PRESENTING PROBLEM	CHEMICAL ABNORMALITIES
Triose phosphate isomerase deficiency	Bulbar signs, hypotonia, non-spherocytic anemia in infancy	Deficient triose phosphate isomerase
Chediak-Higashi syndrome	Peripheral neuropathy, hepatosplenomegaly, lymphadenopathy, malignancies, granules in leukocytes	
Neuroaxonal dystrophy	Peripheral neuropathy, ataxia, bulbar signs, optic atrophy, nystagmus	
Diffuse sclerosis with meningeal angiomatosis	No cutaneous signs	
Lafora's disease (Unverricht's myoclonic epilepsy)	Ataxia, rigidity, blindness	
Lesch-Nyhan syndrome (hyperuricemia)	Sex-linked transmission; choreoathetosis, self-mutilation	Deficient hypoxanthine-guanine phosphoribosyl transferase; elevated serum uric acid
Subcortical (Basal Ganglia) Gray Matter Degenerative Disease	Progressive upper motor neuron impairment with evidence of basal ganglia dysfunction	
Familial striatal degeneration		
Hallervorden-Spatz disease	Myoclonus, optic atrophy	
Hepatolenticular degeneration (Wilson's disease)	Copper deposition in cornea (Kayser-Fleischer ring); hepatic cirrhosis (usually little dementia)	Elevated serum copper; low ceruloplasmin
Pseudo Wilson's disease	Tremor, paresis, vertical eye movements, ataxia, splenomegaly, thrombocytopenia	Abnormal copper kinetic studies
Juvenile Parkinson's disease	Dominant genetic transmission; oculogyria	
Huntington's chorea	Dominant transmission, seizures, ataxia (rigidity most common in childhood)	

TABLE 5 (CONT.)

Fahr's disease	Dominant transmission, ataxia, seizures, calcification of basal ganglia	
Cerebellar Degenerations	Progressive cerebellar dysfunction	
Olivopontocerebellar degeneration	Dominant transmission, retinal degeneration, rigidity	
A-β-lipoproteinemia (Bassen-Kornzweig syndrome)	Posterior column impairment, peripheral neuropathy, retinitis pigmentosa	Decreased serum β-lipoprotein, acanthocytes
Neurocutaneous Syndromes	Associated skin abnormalities	
Neurofibromatosis (von Recklinghausen's disease)	Dominant transmission; café-au-lait spots, neurofibromas subcutaneously, seizures, intracranial tumors and congenital effects	
Tuberous sclerosis (Bourneville's disease)	Café-au-lait or depigmented spots on skin, adenoma sebaceum on face; seizures; intracranial calcification; brain cytoarchitectural changes; tumors of heart, kidney, brain	
Sturge-Weber syndrome	Hemangioma on face with ipsilateral venous angioma over cortex; seizures; contralateral visual and motor deficits; glaucoma; cortical calcification	
Cerebroretinal arteriovenous malformation (Wyburn-Mason syndrome)	Facial, retinal, and brain vascular malformation (particularly brainstem)	
Lindau-von Hippel syndrome	Angiomas of retina; cerebellar hemangioblastoma; cysts of kidney, liver, pancreas	
Ataxia-telangiectasia	Scleral telangiectasia, café-au-lait spots, progressive ataxia, recurrent pneumonia	IgA deficiency
Incontinentia pigmenti (Block-Sulzberger syndrome)	Linear streaking and whorls on skin, dystrophy of fingernails, alopecia, seizures	
Linear sebaceous nevus, nevus unius lateralis, nevi of Ota	Variants of skin nevi on face in association with seizures, eye changes, intracranial tumors	

TABLE 6

Laboratory Studies in Progressive Neurologic Diseases Associated with Mental Deficiency

LABORATORY TESTS	MAJOR CLINICAL FEATURE	DISEASE CATEGORY
EEG	Seizures	
Electromyography, nerve velocity conduction	Peripheral neuropathy, hypotonia	Glycogen storage; white matter disease; lipid storage
Hemogram	Thrombocytopenia, neutropenia, erythrocytes, leukocyte granules	Aminoacidopathies (with metabolic acidosis); cerebellar degenerative diseases; Chediak-Higashi
Routine serum chemistries (thyroid studies, calcium, phosphorus, lipoproteins, adrenal studies, fasting blood sugar, glucose tolerance tests, uric acid, ammonia, liver profile, pyruvic acid, lactic acid, pH, ceruloplasmin, copper)	Associated diseases of other organ systems; hypoglycemia; cortical blindness; self-mutilation; recurrent encephalopathy; dyskinesia	Thyroid deficiency, adreno-leukodystrophy, hypoglycemia, Lesch-Nyhan syndrome, aminoacidopathies (urea cycle, metabolic acidosis), Wilson's disease, cerebellar degeneration, kinky-hair disease
X-rays: skull, spine, extremities	Macrocrania, microcrania, cutaneous abnormalities, grotesque facies, spine and extremity deformities	Mucopolysaccharidoses, mucolipidoses, neurocutaneous disorders, Fahr's disease
Urinary screening studies (ferric chloride, cyanide nitroprusside, dinitrophenylhydrazine, sugar screening, mucopolysaccharide screening)	Presumed metabolic derangement	Aminoacidopathies, mucopolysaccharidoses, carbohydrate disorders
Serum and urine chromatography	Metabolic disorders	Aminoacidopathies, mucopolysaccharidoses, carbohydrate disorders
Enzyme studies (fibroblast, leukocyte, erythrocyte, tissue)	Enzymatic defects	Aminoacidopathies, lipid storage diseases, carbohydrate disorders, mucopolysaccharidoses, mucolipidoses
Morphologic study of biopsied tissue (brain, peripheral nerve, rectal mucosa, liver, kidney, bone marrow, tooth)	Specific storage characteristics, nonspecific disease	All progressive illnesses